Collocations Extra

Multi-level activities for natural English

Elizabeth Walter and Kate Woodford

CAMBRIDGE
UNIVERSITY PRESS

CAMBRIDGE UNIVERSITY PRESS
Cambridge, New York, Melbourne, Madrid, Cape Town, Singapore, São Paulo, Delhi

Cambridge University Press
The Edinburgh Building, Cambridge CB2 8RU, UK

www.cambridge.org
Information on this title: www.cambridge.org/9780521745222
© Cambridge University Press 2010

First published 2010

Printed in the United Kingdom at the University Press, Cambridge

A catalogue record for this publication is available from the British Library

ISBN 978-0-521-74522-2

Contents

Map of the book

Unit number and title	Level	Activity type	Example collocations	Time
1 Everyday activities				
1.1 What we do	Elementary / Pre-intermediate	Questionnaire	read the paper, watch television, clean your teeth	35–45 mins
1.2 The routines game	Intermediate	Board game	lay the table, make the bed, fall asleep	45 mins
1.3 A day in the life	Advanced	Text substitution Completing word forks	call in sick, pick up a bargain, get off to sleep	45 mins
2 Families and relationships				
2.1 This is your life	Elementary / Pre-intermediate	Story telling	make friends, best friend, big family, happy marriage	45 mins – 1 hour
2.2 Best of friends	Intermediate	Discussion	get in touch, form a friendship, warm welcome	45 mins – 1 hour
2.3 Love Story	Advanced	Crossword Jigsaw reading	propose marriage, fairytale wedding, gain custody	45 mins – 1 hour
3 Communicating				
3.1 It's good to talk	Elementary / Pre-intermediate	Class survey	get a text, have a chat, make a phone call	30–40 mins
3.2 Talking sense	Intermediate	Auction Questionnaire	tell the truth, tell a lie, tell a story	40–45 mins
3.3 You're making it up!	Advanced	Definitions game	sweeping generalisation, rash promise, feeble excuse	45 mins
4 Describing people				
4.1 Who am I?	Elementary / Pre-intermediate	Board game	curly hair, wear glasses, have a beard	40–50 mins
4.2 Wanted!	Intermediate	Writing descriptions	broad shoulders, bald patch, heavy build	45 mins
4.3 Find a friend	Advanced	Reading Discussion Writing	outgoing personality, keen interest, deeply religious	45 mins – 1 hour
5 Emotions and feelings				
5.1 Feelings	Elementary / Pre-intermediate	Matching sentences Sentence completion	feel angry/bored, make *someone* sad/happy	45 mins
5.2 Consequences	Intermediate	Gap fill sentences Playing Consequences	be in a good mood, hurt *someone's* feelings, be worried sick	45 mins – 1 hour
5.3 Dominoes	Advanced	Dominoes Text substitution	bitterly disappointed, blissfully happy, mildly irritated	45 mins

Unit number and title	Level	Activity type	Example collocations	Time
6 Studying and learning				
6.1 A life of learning	Elementary / Pre-intermediate	Information gap	go to school, do your homework, take an exam	45–50 mins
6.2 Which school?	Intermediate	Reading Discussion Writing	continue your studies, get bored, quick learner	45 mins – 1 hour
6.3 A good education	Advanced	Reading Ordering sentences Discussion	background reading, room for improvement, attend lectures	40–50 mins
7 Problems and solutions				
7.1 A bad day	Elementary / Pre-intermediate	Matching collocations Ordering pictures to tell a story	late for work, lose your house keys, miss the train	40–50 mins
7.2 If I were you …	Intermediate	Categorising Giving advice	consider a possibility, keep in mind, bear in mind, a range of options	40–50 mins
7.3 Problems at work	Advanced	Categorising Making recommendations	poor performance, high absence rates, unprofessional attitude	45 mins – 1 hour
8 Food and drink				
8.1 Going shopping	Elementary / Pre-intermediate	Picture matching Board game Talking about food	bar of chocolate, bunch of grapes, packet of biscuits	40–50 mins
8.2 Let's cook!	Intermediate	Ordering texts Mime Describing recipes	melt the chocolate, chop the onions, sift the flour	45 mins – 1 hour
8.3 Restaurant reviews	Advanced	Jigsaw reading Writing reviews	limp salad, crisp pastry, soggy vegetables	45 mins – 1 hour
9 Travel				
9.1 Travel survey	Elementary / Pre-intermediate	Class survey	catch a bus, go by train, ride a bike	45 mins
9.2 Going for a drive	Intermediate	Bingo Writing	heavy traffic, change gear, dip your headlights	45 mins – 1 hour
9.3 Further afield	Advanced	Reading Writing clues Board game	internal flight, long-haul flight, travel light	45 mins – 1 hour
10 Health and medicine				
10.1 Doctor, doctor	Elementary / Pre-intermediate	Board game	call an ambulance, have an operation, take a tablet	40–50 mins
10.2 In good health	Intermediate	Jigsaw reading Role play	fall ill, sharp pain, sore throat	40–50 mins
10.3 A healthy mind	Advanced	Crossword	symptoms persist, undergo treatment, in a critical condition	45 mins – 1 hour

Map of the book

Unit number and title	Level	Activity type	Example collocations	Time
11 Work				
11.1 The world of work	Elementary / Pre-intermediate	Board game	look for a job, earn money, work hard	40–50 mins
11.2 Overworked?	Intermediate	Jigsaw reading Writing definitions	heavy workload, long hours, reach a target	30–45 mins
11.3 Work stories	Advanced	Matching collocations and definitions Story writing Mingle	high-powered job, hand in your notice, land a job	45 mins
12 Money				
12.1 Money money money!	Elementary / Pre-intermediate	Discussion Gap fill	borrow money, pay a bill, pay tax	35–45 mins
12.2 Short of money	Intermediate	Finding collocations in texts Giving advice Role play	pay interest, poorly paid, leave a tip, make a living	45 mins
12.3 Good with money?	Advanced	Gap fill Reading Role play	big-ticket item, value for money, hard-earned cash	45 mins
13 Where we live				
13.1 Leaving home	Elementary / Pre-intermediate	Gap fill sentences Discussion Word forks	leave home, feel homesick, do the housework	35–45 mins
13.2 Room to let	Intermediate	Matching collocations and definitions Matching texts Writing advertisements	residential area, fully furnished, friendly neighbourhood	40–50 mins
13.3 A better place to live	Advanced	Reading Role play Preparing a report	antisocial behaviour, underage drinking, littered pavements	45 mins – 1 hour
14 Crime and punishment				
14.1 Call the police!	Elementary / Pre-intermediate	Jigsaw reading Writing crime stories	a serious crime, call the police, police arrest *someone*	45 mins
14.2 We have reached a verdict …	Intermediate	Gap fill Running dictation Writing Discussion and role play	be found guilty, criminal record, plead guilty	45 mins – 1 hour
14.3 Does the punishment fit the crime?	Advanced	Writing two opposing texts Role play	extenuating circumstances, unprovoked attack, hardened criminal	45 mins

Unit number and title	Level	Activity type	Example collocations	Time
15 Modern technology				
15.1 Home computer	Elementary / Pre-intermediate	Gap fill Class survey	send an email, new message, go online	40–50 mins
15.2 Help – it won't work!	Intermediate	Writing definitions Role play	a password expires, delete a file, print out a document	45 mins – 1 hour
15.3 What do you use *yours* for?	Advanced	Categorising Definitions game	download music, back up your work, bookmark a site	45 mins – 1 hour
16 The natural world				
16.1 Wish you were here!	Elementary / Pre-intermediate	Matching collocations Gap fill sentences Writing postcards	sandy beach, bright sunshine, thick fog	40–50 mins
16.2 Disaster!	Intermediate	Reading Running dictation Writing	widespread flooding, bring chaos, rivers burst their banks	45 mins – 1 hour
16.3 Adventure travel	Advanced	Writing definitions Jumbled texts Writing journal entries	hard frost, fast-flowing river, stifling heat	45 mins – 1 hour
17 Sport and exercise				
17.1 What exercise do you do?	Elementary / Pre-intermediate	Listening Class survey	do aerobics, play football, go swimming	45 mins – 1 hour
17.2 The beautiful game	Intermediate	Reading Auction Writing a report	long-range shot, hit the crossbar, gain possession	45 mins – 1 hour
17.3 Champions past and present	Advanced	Text substitution Role play	defend a title, loss of form, reigning champion	45 mins – 1 hour
18 Leisure activities				
18.1 Free-time fun	Elementary / Pre-intermediate	Free-time activity survey	go to a concert, read a book, listen to the radio	45 mins – 1 hour
18.2 Star quality	Intermediate	Reading Writing	star in a film, release an album, direct a movie	45 mins – 1 hour
18.3 Critics' corner	Advanced	Reading Text substitution Writing	bold experiment, compulsive reading, lasting impression	45 mins – 1 hour

Introduction

What is *Collocations Extra*?

Collocations Extra is a resource book containing 54 easy-to-use, self-contained vocabulary lessons for busy teachers. Each lesson consists of one page of step-by-step teacher's notes and a photocopiable worksheet. The worksheets are aimed at young adult (16+) and adult learners. Designed to supplement general English courses and ranging from elementary to advanced level, each lesson presents and practises a set of target collocations through communicative activities for pairs and groups of students. The lessons cover common vocabulary topics, and the collocations are presented in contexts that are both realistic and relevant to students.

How will *Collocations Extra* help my students?

Collocation is the key to a high standard of English. Students need to know the words that operate the vocabulary they have learned, and if they know the combinations that native speakers use – which can often be difficult or impossible to guess – their English will sound natural, fluent and elegant.

This book will help students learn key collocations in topic areas that interest them. Because it teaches the collocations in a clear and thorough way, it will give students the language they need to speak and write about those topics with confidence.

How is *Collocations Extra* organised?

Collocations Extra has 18 units, organised by topic. The units can be used in any order, not necessarily the order in which they appear in this book. The book does not get progressively more difficult. Each unit has three lessons: elementary / pre-intermediate level, intermediate level, and advanced. The lessons consist of one worksheet, accompanied by step-by-step teacher's notes.

The lessons are designed to last between 35 minutes and an hour. Preparation is always minimal. Teachers will need to photocopy worksheets and, in some cases, cut them up before the lesson. Some lessons also require the use of a good learner's dictionary (for example *Cambridge Advanced Learner's Dictionary*).

The teacher's notes include a key information panel for quick reference. The headings in this section are:

Level: Elementary / Pre-intermediate, Intermediate or Advanced.

Activity types: A brief description of the main types of activity in the input, practice and/or follow-up stages.

Materials: everything that will be required for the lesson.

Target collocations: the key language that will be presented and practised in the lesson. Teachers should know which collocations will be targetted before they start the lesson.

Time: approximate timing of all four stages of the lesson. The timing of the follow-up activity is often at the teacher's discretion.

The lessons are divided into four main stages:

- **Warmer:** This is a very short introduction to the topic area, taking only a few minutes and usually not requiring any materials. The warmer often makes use of the students' own personal knowledge and experiences.
- **Input:** One key feature of this book is that it aims to teach collocations in a thorough way. It does not assume that the students know any of the collocations in the unit. The input stage, therefore, is always an activity which explicitly introduces all the lesson's target collocations.
- **Practice:** The practice activity always develops students' understanding of the collocations presented in the input stage. It does this by practising the collocations in controlled contexts, using communicative pair or group work.

- **Follow-up:** The final activity allows students to use the collocations they have learned in a freer way, often giving them the opportunity to bring in other vocabulary and ideas.

At the beginning of the book you will find a 'map' which gives an overview of the topic, activity type and example collocations for each lesson.

At the back there is a full list of all the collocations in the book, organised by topic and level.

CD-ROM

The *Collocations Extra* CD-ROM allows you to create games for further practice of the target collocations in each unit. Simply choose a unit topic and a level, and decide whether you would like your students to play Dominoes, Pelmanism or What's the Collocation? The CD-ROM will then instantly generate a worksheet for you to print out and cut up. For details about which of the games are most appropriate for each unit, refer to the table on pages 125–126.

Thanks and acknowledgements

The authors and publishers are grateful to the following people who reviewed and piloted the material with their students during its development:

Elizabeth Babenko, Kazakhstan

Philip Dale, UK

Maria Davou, UK

Jackie Harsall, UK

Garan Holcombe, UK

Andrew Scott, Australia

Rui da Silva, UK

Cristina Zurawski Biriescu, USA

The authors would like to thank everyone at Cambridge University Press who has been involved in the development of this book. In particular, thanks are due to Caroline Thiriau, who developed the idea for this book and whose support and advice in its early stages were invaluable; to Frances Disken who has provided continual help, encouragement and an eagle editorial eye throughout the writing stage; to Ian Collier and Nikolaos Kovaios who were responsible for development of the CD-ROM, and to Nóirín Burke, who oversaw everything with her usual calm efficiency. We would also like to thank Karen Jamieson for the excellent work she did in preparing the final manuscript for production; and Lizzie Geldart for stepping in to see the book successfully through the proof stages.

Illustrations: Mark Duffin (pp.55, 57, 77); David Mostyn (pp.31, 49, 69, 75); Javier Joaquin (pp.33, 67, 105); Sam Thompson (pp.19, 37, 53, 103); Vicky Woodgate (pp.13, 109).

Text design: Kamae Design

Page make-up: Kamae Design

1.1

What we do

LEVEL
Elementary /
Pre-intermediate

ACTIVITY TYPE
Questionnaire

MATERIALS
One copy of the
worksheet for each
student

**TARGET
COLLOCATIONS**

call a friend,
catch the bus,
clean your teeth,
have a shower,
have breakfast,
listen to music,
make dinner,
meet a friend,
read the paper,
watch television

TIME
35–45 minutes

Warmer

1   Put students in pairs. Ask each pair to write a list of six things they do every day. Explain that the first pair to write six appropriate things is the winner.

2   Feed back, checking that the winners' answers are correct.

Input

1   Give each student a copy of the worksheet, folded in two vertically so only the pictures are showing. Put students in pairs to identify what is happening in the pictures.

2   Elicit the target collocations, and write them on the board.

Practice

1   Ask students to unfold their worksheets. Explain that they should complete the sentences with the names of other students in the class by asking questions to find out which things the students do. Explain that they should have a different name in each sentence. Elicit what the question form would be *Do you ...?* and demonstrate asking the question.

2   When the students have finished, conduct feedback by asking students to read out some of their sentences, e.g. *Philip never has breakfast*.

Follow-up

1   Ask each student to write two true things and one false thing about what they do in a typical day or week.

2   In pairs, have students read their sentences to each other, and the listener must guess which statement is false.

🌐 See page 125–6 for the best games from the CD-ROM to play after this unit.

FIND SOMEONE WHO ...

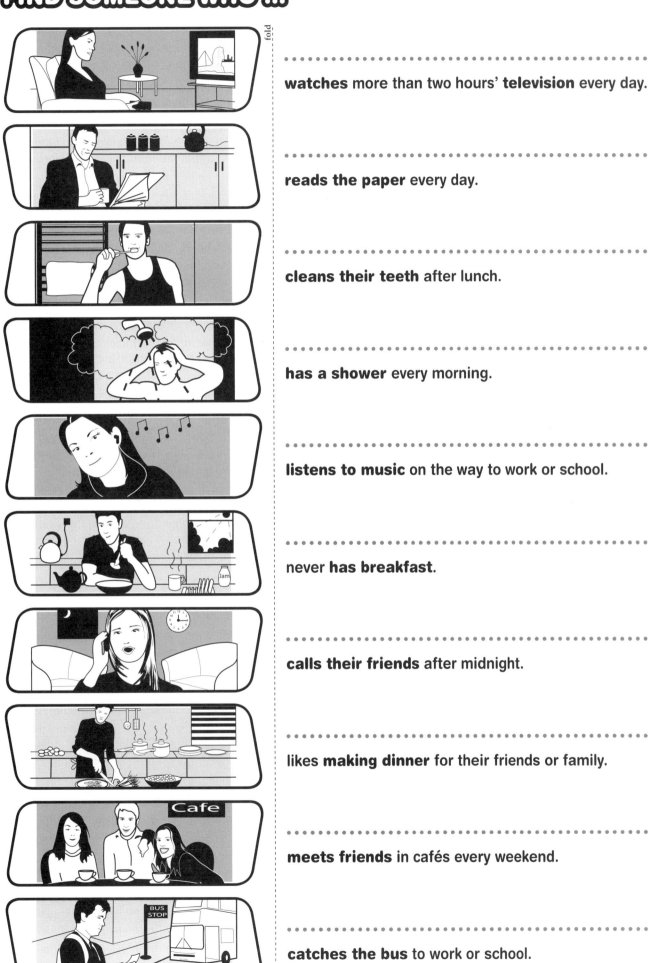

watches more than two hours' **television** every day.

reads the paper every day.

cleans their teeth after lunch.

has a shower every morning.

listens to music on the way to work or school.

never **has breakfast**.

calls their friends after midnight.

likes **making dinner** for their friends or family.

meets friends in cafés every weekend.

catches the bus to work or school.

1.2

The routines game

LEVEL
Intermediate

ACTIVITY TYPE
Board game

MATERIALS
One copy of the worksheet, and a coin for each group of 3–5 students
One counter for each student

TARGET COLLOCATIONS
check your email,
do the housework,
do the ironing,
do the washing-up,
draw the curtains,
fall asleep,
get dressed/ undressed,
go out for dinner,
lay the table,
lock the door,
make the bed,
open the blinds,
pay the bills,
turn on the TV

TIME
45 minutes

Warmer

1   Write the words *daily routine* on the board and ask the students if they know what this means. Explain that it means *all the things you usually do during the day*. Tell the students that you are going to be talking about things that you do every day.

2   Put students in pairs and ask them to think of all the things that they usually do in a typical day. Give them three minutes to write as many things as they can. The winners are the pair with the most things.

Input

1   Put students in groups of 3–5. Give each group a photocopy of the board game on the worksheet. Ask the students to match the words dotted around the board with the words on the board to form collocations.

2   Conduct feedback, and have students make a note of the collocations.

Practice

1   Explain the rules of the game:

   ● Students take turns to toss a coin and move their counters around the board: heads = one square, tails = two squares (do not count a square if another player's counter is already on it).

   ● When players land on a square, they must make a question using one of the sentence heads in the middle of the board, the word on their square and a collocating word from around the edge of the board. They then ask this question to the person on their left. Explain that they can add an extra word or phrase to their question to make it work (e.g. *Who gets dressed first in the morning in your house?*).

   ● Before that player answers, the other players in the game have to check that the question is meaningful (e.g. You might say, *Have you ever fallen asleep in a lesson?*, but not *have you ever fallen asleep?*). If the question is not meaningful, the player must go back one square and then it's the turn of the player on the left. If it is meaningful, the player on the left should answer the question, and then take their turn to toss the coin.

   ● Play continues until one player reaches the Finish square.

2   When the students have finished playing the game, conduct feedback by asking the teams for any interesting information they found out.

Follow-up

Put students in pairs. They should choose five things that they both do at least once a week and write sentences using these word partners.

See page 125–6 for the best games from the CD-ROM to play after this unit.

check

lay

make

get

fall

go out for

email	door	TV	washing-up
dressed	*Have you ever …?*		housework
blinds	*When did you last …?* *Who … in your house?*		bills
table	*Do you like …?*		curtains
FINISH	*How often do you …?* *Have you ever forgotten to …?*		undressed
START	bed	dinner	asleep	ironing

do

pay

open

turn on

lock

draw

1.3

A day in the life

LEVEL
Advanced

ACTIVITY TYPE
Text substitution
Completing word
forks

MATERIALS
One copy of the
worksheet for each
pair

**TARGET
COLLOCATIONS**
alarm clock goes
off,
call in sick,
catch up on sleep,
clear up a mess,
get off to sleep,
pick up a bargain,
soak up the sun,
stay out late,
strike up a
conversation,
work up an
appetite

TIME
45 minutes

Warmer

1   Put students in pairs.

2   Ask each pair to tell each other what they did yesterday. Give each student one minute to explain everything that they did the previous day.

Input

1   Give each pair a copy of the worksheet.

2   Ask each pair to read the text *My day* from the worksheet and replace the words in italics with a phrasal verb from the list (making any necessary changes to the verb).

> **Answer key**
> **1** called in   **2** going off   **3** cleared up   **4** pick up   **5** struck up   **6** soaked up
> **7** work up   **8** stay out   **9** catch up on   **10** get off

3   Refer students to the word forks on the worksheet. Have them fill in the collocations they have just learned from the text in the appropriate places (they do this by deciding if the verbs also collocate with the words already set in the word fork).

4   Elicit/explain the meanings of the new collocations.

> **Answer key**
> **1**   catch up on *sleep/work*
> **2**   clear up *any confusion / a mess*
> **3**   pick up *a friend from the station / a bargain*
> **4**   soak up *the atmosphere / the sun*
> **5**   work up *an appetite / a sweat*

Practice

1   Have students work individually or in pairs to write a paragraph using five of the collocations.

2   Ask students to tell their stories to each other. They should listen out for the collocations, checking that they have been used appropriately.

Follow-up

1   Put students in pairs. Ask each pair to choose five collocations which describe activities that they do and to write them down. Explain that they should also rank the activities (in secret) from one to five in order of preference, one being the activity they like best, five being the activity they like least.

2   Explain that each person should tell their partner the five collocations they have chosen, and should ask their partner to guess the order in which they ranked them.

3   After each student has guessed the other's ranking, they should explain their likes and dislikes to each other.

⊙ See page 125–6 for the best games from the CD-ROM to play after this unit.

A Replace the words in italics in the text with a phrasal verb from the list below.

| catch up on | clear up | strike up | call in | pick up | get off | go off | soak up | stay out | work up |

My day

Yesterday when I woke I just couldn't face the thought of another day in the office so I did something I've never done before. I [1] *phoned the office* to say I was sick. As I crept back upstairs to my bedroom I could hear my flatmate Alice's alarm clock [2] *making a noise*. I presumed she was still fast asleep so I knocked on her door then got myself ready for the day. I went to the kitchen and [3] *tidied* the mess from the previous night (we'd had friends over for dinner). After a quick breakfast I caught a bus into town. I thought I'd check out the sales and see if I could [4] *get* any bargains. While I was on the bus I [5] *started* a conversation with a girl who told me which sales to go to. After a bit of shopping, I ate a sandwich in the park and [6] *enjoyed* the sun for an hour or so. After that I decided to go for a walk to [7] *give me more of* an appetite for dinner with Alice later in the evening. We met at 7:00, a little early for dinner but I didn't want to [8] *be in town till* late. Besides, I'd been out a lot lately and wanted to [9] *get* some sleep. In fact, when I did get to bed my mind was racing and I didn't [10] *manage to go* to sleep till gone two o'clock.

B Complete the word forks with collocations from the text.

1 ....
- ....
- work

2 ....
- any confusion
- a ....

3 ....
- a friend from the station
- a ....

4 ....
- the atmosphere
- the ....

5 ....
- an ....
- a sweat

2.1

This is your life

LEVEL
Elementary /
Pre-intermediate

ACTIVITY TYPE
Story telling

MATERIALS
One set of the
pictures and
collocations (Part A
of the worksheet)
for each pair
One story (Part B)
for each student
One set of questions
(Part C) cut up into
slips for each
student

**TARGET
COLLOCATIONS**
best friend,
big family,
fall in love,
get divorced,
get married,
happy marriage,
have children,
leave home,
live together,
make friends

TIME
45 minutes – 1 hour

Warmer

1 Put students in two teams (one called *friend* and one called *family*) and ask each team to line up in front of the board.

2 Write *friend* in large letters on the board in front of the *friend* team, and *family* in large letters in front of the *family* team. Give a board pen to the person at the front of each line. Explain that when you say *go* they should write a word beginning with *f* vertically down from the *f* in *family* or *friend* (depending on which team they belong to).

3 They should then give the pen to the next person in their team, who should write a word beginning with *r* down from the *r* in *friend*, if they are in the *friend team,* or a word beginning with *a* down from the *a* in *family* if they are in the *family team*.

4 The game continues until one of the teams has one word descending from each of the letters in their word.

Input

1 Put students in pairs. Ask each pair to look at the pictures and the collocations (Part A of the worksheet) and match the collocations to the pictures.

2 Check the answers and make sure everyone understands the collocations.

> **Answer key**
> **1** make friends **2** best friends **3** big family **4** leave home **5** fall in love
> **6** live together **7** get married **8** happy marriage **9** have children
> **10** get divorced

Practice

1 Give each pair a copy of the story (Part B of the worksheet). Explain that they should fill in the gaps with the collocations (putting the verbs in the correct form where necessary).

2 Check answers.

3 Give each pair a second copy of the story. Ask student A in each pair to read the story out loud using the version with gaps, but completing the sentences as they read. Student B should check, using the completed story, that student A uses the collocations correctly.

4 Have student A and B switch roles and repeat step three.

5 As a final stage, give students some time to try and commit the story to memory. Then, repeat steps 3 and 4, but this time have one student look at the completed story, and have the other student look only at the pictures and collocations.

Variation

If you have a very strong class, have them write their own story using the collocations and the pictures only.

Follow-up

1 Give each student one of the question slips (Part C of the worksheet). Have them move around the classroom, asking each other the questions.

2 Conduct feedback, asking the students to tell the class some of the most interesting answers.

● See page 125–6 for the best games from the CD-ROM to play after this unit.

A Match the pictures below and the collocations in the box.

| best friends | big family | fall in love | get divorced | get married | happy marriage | have children |
| leave home | live together | make friends | | | | |

1   2   3   4   5

6   7   8   9   10

B Complete the story with the collocations (putting the verbs in the correct form where necessary).

STORY

Kitty always enjoyed school. She .... lots of .... there. Her .... was Amy. Amy did not have any brothers and sisters, but Kitty had a ...., and there was always a lot of noise and fun in their house.

Kitty .... when she was 18, to go to university. There she met Marc, and they .... After university, they .... for a few years, and then they ....

At first, they had a very ...., and soon they .... two .... Unfortunately, they started to have problems. After a few years, Kitty told Marc to leave, and they ....

C Questions

What is a good way to make friends?	What is the best age to leave home?
Why do people get divorced?	What is the best way to have a happy marriage?
What is the best age to have children?	Why do people fall in love?

2.2

Best of friends

LEVEL
Intermediate

ACTIVITY TYPE
Discussion

MATERIALS
One copy of the collocations (Part A of the worksheet) for each student
One copy of the questions (Part B) for each student

TARGET COLLOCATIONS
circle of friends,
close family,
close friend,
enjoy *someone's* company,
form a friendship,
frosty reception,
get in touch,
keep in touch,
lose touch,
old friend,
stay in touch,
warm welcome

TIME
45 minutes to 1 hour

Warmer

Write the phrase *blood is thicker than water* on the board. Elicit/explain what it means (it means that family relationships are stronger and more important than any other relationships), and ask students if they agree. Explain that in this lesson you are going to talk about friends.

Input

1 Put students in pairs. Give each pair a copy of the collocations (Part A of the worksheet).
2 Ask students to identify the one pair of collocations that have the same meaning. Then have them discuss the difference between the other pairs of collocations.
3 Give out the remaining copies of Part A so that each student has a copy.
4 Check answers.

> **Answer key**
>
> 1 *close friends – close family*: These are similar in that you have a good relationship with both of these, but of course you are related to family, but not to friends.
> 2 *circle of friends – old friends*: Your circle of friends is all the people who are your friends. Old friends are people who have been your friends for a long time.
> 3 *keep in touch – stay in touch*: These mean the same – to continue to have contact with someone.
> 4 *enjoy someone's company – form a close friendship*: If you enjoy someone's company, you like being with them, but you only form a close friendship if you both mutually like and trust each other very much.
> 5 *lose touch – get in touch*: If you lose touch with someone, you stop having contact with them, but if you get in touch, you make contact with them.
> 6 *warm welcome – frosty reception*: If you give someone a warm welcome, you show that you are very pleased to see them, but if you give them a frosty reception, you show that you are not pleased to see them.

Practice

1 Give each pair a copy of the questions (Part B of the worksheet).
2 Put students in pairs. Have them discuss the questions.
3 Give out the remaining copies of Part B so that each student has a copy.
4 Conduct feedback.

Follow-up

1 Tell the students they are now going to do a class survey using the questions (Part B). Put students in groups of four and have them divide the questions between them (so each has two to three questions). Then have them ask everyone in the class their questions, keeping a note of the results.
2 At the end, ask each group to write up their results to be displayed in the class.

⦿ See page 125–6 for the best games from the CD-ROM to play after this unit.

A Look at the pairs of collocations. In which pair do both the phrases have the same meaning? What are the differences between the phrases in the other pairs of collocations?

1 close friends / close family

2 circle of friends / old friends

3 keep in touch / stay in touch

4 enjoy someone's company / form a close friendship

5 lose touch / get in touch

6 warm welcome / frosty reception

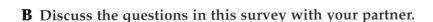

B Discuss the questions in this survey with your partner.

Survey

1 Is it more important to have close family or close friends?

2 What's the best way of keeping in touch with your friends?

3 What is the best way to increase your circle of friends?

4 Is it a good idea to form a close friendship with your next-door neighbour?

5 Do you always give a warm welcome to visitors to your house? Does anyone ever get a frosty reception?

6 Why do you think so many people lose touch with their school friends?

7 Is it worth trying to stay in touch with old friends when you don't share many interests with them any more?

8 What really makes you enjoy someone's company?

9 If you lose contact with someone, what's the best way to get in touch again?

2.3

LEVEL
Advanced

ACTIVITY TYPE
Crossword
Jigsaw reading

MATERIALS
One copy of the crossword (Part A of the worksheet) for each student
Either the 'Hannah' or the 'Martin' text (Part B) for each person in a pair
A photo of a couple clearly in love

TARGET COLLOCATIONS
end in divorce,
fairytale wedding,
fight for custody,
gain custody,
immediate family,
love at first sight,
messy divorce,
mutual friend,
pay maintenance,
propose marriage,
set up home,
throw a party

TIME
45 minutes – 1 hour

Love story

Warmer

Show the class a picture of a couple who are clearly in love. Ask the class what good or bad things might happen in their relationship.

Input

1   Put students in pairs. Give each pair a copy of the crossword (Part A of the worksheet). Have the students complete it together.

2   Give out the remaining copies of the crossword so that each student has a copy. Check answers, and make sure everyone understands the collocations.

> **Answer key**
>
> **Across: 3** home   **5** friend   **6** sight   **8** marriage   **9** wedding   **11** family
> **Down: 1** throw   **2** divide   **4** custody   **7** gained   **8** messy   **10** map

Practice

1   Have students work individually. Give half the class Hannah's story and half the class Martin's story (Part B of the worksheet). Have the students read the stories for gist to find out what happens.

2   When the students have finished reading, pair up each student who has read Hannah's text with a student who has read Martin's text.

3   Refer students back to the crossword clues from the input stage. Have the students discuss, according to what they have read, which of the sentences are true, and whose story (Hannah's or Martin's) gives evidence for this.

4   Conduct whole-class feedback, drawing out the key differences between the two texts.

> **Answer key**
>
> **Across: 3** true   **5** true   **6** true   **8** true   **9** false   **10** false   **11** Hannah says this is true, Martin says it is false
> **Down: 1** false   **2** true   **4** false   **7** true   **8** false   **10** false

Follow-up

1   Tell the class to imagine they are taking part in a reality TV chat show. In this show a presenter speaks to guests with problems, and the audience gives advice and opinions and asks questions. Allow two minutes for each student to invent a problem (e.g. they might disagree with their wife/husband on how to bring up their children, or they may have got into debt).

2   Play the role of the presenter yourself. Ask each student in turn to explain their problem and invite the audience to offer their opinions. Chair the discussion, encouraging debate and discussion amongst the audience.

● See page 125–6 for the best games from the CD-ROM to play after this unit.

A Complete the crossword.

Across

3 The couple decided to **set up h**............... together in Paris.

5 They were introduced by a **mutual f**................

6 For him, it was **love at first s**................ .

8 After a year, he **proposed m**................ .

9 They had a **fairytale w**............... in Italy.

11 They only invited their **immediate f**............... to their wedding.

Down

1 They decided to **t**............... **a party** for all their friends.

2 Their marriage **ended in d**............... after five years.

4 He decided to **fight for c**............... of the children.

7 She **g**............... **custody** of the children.

8 It was a particularly **m**............... **divorce**.

10 He refuses to **p**............... **maintenance** for his children.

✂---

B There are always two sides to a story ...

Hannah

'I met Martin when we were both art students in Paris. He always said that for him it was **love at first sight**. I wasn't sure at first, but he was charming and fun to be with, and my feelings for him grew. So when he **proposed marriage** after we'd been together for a year, I was delighted.

'I had always dreamed of a **fairytale wedding**, but Martin said it was a waste of money. So in the end we had a small party for our **immediate family** in London.

'We **set up home** in Paris and it went downhill from there. Martin demanded to know exactly what I spent my money on. After we had children, things became even worse. I gave up work to look after them, and Martin refused to give me any money for myself. We argued about money all the time. Five years after our wedding, the marriage **ended in divorce**.

'The only good thing was that I knew Martin would never **fight for custody** of the children – he's too mean to pay a lawyer! So at least it wasn't a **messy divorce**. He hardly ever comes to see them, but at least he manages to **pay** the **maintenance**.'

✂---

There are always two sides to a story ...

Martin

'I met Hannah when we were both art students in Paris. A **mutual friend** introduced us and it was **love at first sight** for both of us. She was very beautiful in those days, and I could see that other men were jealous when they saw me with her. When we'd been together for a year, I **proposed marriage**.

'Our first major argument was over the wedding. Hannah's plans for a **fairytale wedding** would have left us in debt for years. I talked her out of that, but she still insisted on **throwing a** lavish **party** for her enormous family in London.

'We **set up home** in a suburb of Paris but it was a disaster. Hannah was useless with money, especially after the children arrived, and we argued constantly. I don't know how the marriage lasted five years.

'After the divorce, Hannah **gained custody** of the children, of course. I didn't fight the decision, as a **messy divorce** would have been bad for the children. Now they live on the other side of Paris and I only see them once a month – I have to **pay** so much **maintenance** that I can't afford the train fare any more often than that.'

3.1

It's good to talk

LEVEL
Elementary /
Pre-intermediate

ACTIVITY TYPE
Class survey

MATERIALS
One copy of the
word spiral (Part A
of the worksheet)
for each student
One copy of the
class survey (Part B)
for each student

**TARGET
COLLOCATIONS**
get a letter,
get a phone call,
get a text,
get an email,
have a chat,
have an argument,
make a phone call,
send a letter,
send a text
send an email,

TIME
30–40 minutes

Warmer

1 Put students in pairs. Give each pair a copy of the word spiral and word forks (Part A of the worksheet). Explain that there are six nouns related to communication in the spiral. Students should find the nouns.

2 Check answers and write them on the board.

> **Answer key**
> chat, argument, letter, email, phone call, text

3 Give out the remaining copies of Part A so that each student has a copy.

Input

Refer students to the word forks. Have them complete the word forks with the nouns from the spiral.

> **Answer key**
> *have* a chat / an argument
> *make* a phone call
> *send* a letter / a text / an email
> *get* a letter / a text / an email / a phone call

Practice

1 Give each student a copy of the class survey (Part B of the worksheet).

2 Model the first question *How often do you send an email* and elicit answers (*every day; once / twice / three times a week / a day / a month / an hour; never,* etc.).

3 Ask students to write the names of the other people in their class at the top of the columns on the questionnaire. Have the students mingle and interview everyone in the class, writing down their answers (*never, once a week,* etc.) in the appropriate box.

4 Conduct feedback by asking students to compare their answers with a partner and choose three interesting facts from the survey to report back to the class.

Follow-up

Ask students in pairs to tell each other five things that they did yesterday using the collocations they have learned. They should say, where appropriate, how often they did those things.

⊕ See page 125–6 for the best games from the CD-ROM to play after this unit.

A Word spiral

There are six communication words here. Can you find them?

have
• a ....
• an ....

make ——— • a ....

send
• a ....
• a ....
• an ....

get
• a ....
• a ....
• an ....
• a ....

---✂--

B Class survey

How often do you ...?

Activities:	Names:							
send an email								
send a letter								
send a text								
get an email								
get a letter								
get a text								
get a phone call								
make a phone call								
have a chat with a friend								
have an argument with a friend								

3.2

Talking sense

LEVEL
Intermediate

ACTIVITY TYPE
Auction
Questionnaire

MATERIALS
One copy of the gap
fill sentences (Part A
of the worksheet)
for each student
One copy of the
auction
questionnaire (Part
B) for each student

**TARGET
COLLOCATIONS**
say goodbye,
say hello,
say sorry,
say your prayers,
speak your mind,
talk nonsense,
talk sense,
tell a joke,
tell a lie,
tell a story,
tell the truth

TIME
40–45 minutes

Warmer

1   Write the following anagrams on the board: *ysa*, *ktla*, *ksepa*, *ltle*.

2   Ask the students to unravel the anagrams, telling them that each word is a verb, and that all of them have similar meanings.

> **Answer key**
> say, talk, speak, tell

Input

1   Put students in pairs. Give each pair a copy of the gap fill sentences (Part A of the worksheet).

2   Have students work in pairs to complete the sentences with the appropriate word from the anagrams task in the Warmer above.

3   Give out the remaining copies of the gap fill so that each student has one. Check answers.

> **Answer key**
> **1** tell   **2** says/said   **3** talking   **4** speak   **5** say   **6** tell   **7** say   **8** telling
> **9** said   **10** tell   **11** talks

Practice

1   Make sure that the students can't see their gap fills from the previous activity. (You may like to collect these in while you do this activity.)

2   Discuss with the class what happens at an auction, teaching the phrasal verb *bid for something* or the phrase *make a bid for something*.

3   Put students in pairs. Tell them that each pair has £5000 (or the equivalent in their currency, if you are teaching a monolingual class) to spend at an auction. The lowest acceptable bid is £200. They have to try to buy as many correct questions as possible and should only bid for questions they believe are correct.

4   Give each pair a copy of the auction questionnaire (Part B of the worksheet). Have them decide on their maximum bid for each question, writing it in the first column.

5   To begin the auction, read out the questions one at a time, and ask for bids. Sell each question to the highest bidder. Ask the highest bidder to note down in the second column how much they have paid.

6   When all the questions have been sold, go through the list and tell students whether each question was correct or not. Elicit the correct form where the question is incorrect.

7   The winners are the pair who have bought the most correct questions.

8   Give out the remaining copies of the auction questionnaires so that each student has a copy. Have all the students mark the corrections on their questionnaires.

> **Answer key**
> **1** *tell* stories   **2** *talk/speak* nonsense   **3** *speak your* mind   **4** *say* sorry
> **5** *tell* a joke   **6** *tell* a lie

Follow-up

1   Have each pair ask and answer the questions for themselves.

2   Conduct feedback, asking students to report back any interesting responses.

⊙ See page 125–6 for the best games from the CD-ROM to play after this unit.

A Work in pairs to complete the sentences with the appropriate word.

1   My grandfather used to .... us wonderful **stories** when we were children.

2   She .... her **prayers** before bedtime every night.

3   He's .... **nonsense** – I've never heard such rubbish in my life.

4   She's not afraid to .... **her mind** – if she thinks you're doing something wrong, she will tell you.

5   Grandma is leaving now, Charlie, come and .... **goodbye** to her.

6   .... **the truth** – do I look silly in this hat?

7   I wanted to .... **sorry** to her for upsetting her.

8   She was .... **jokes** to the children, trying to make them laugh.

9   I .... **hello** but I didn't have time to talk to her properly.

10   He would never .... a **lie** – he's extremely honest.

11   I don't admire many politicians but I admire him – he .... a lot of **sense**.

✂--

B Sentences for auction

	Which sentences are correct?	Maximum bid	Price paid
1	Can you say stories without reading them from a book?		
2	Can you name four different places where people say their prayers?		
3	Do you think all politicians say nonsense?		
4	Do you always speak the mind?		
5	Can you say hello and goodbye in six languages?		
6	Do you find it hard to tell sorry?		
7	Can you say a joke in English?		
8	Do you always tell the truth?		
9	Do you think it is OK to speak a lie in some situations?		
10	Can you name a politician who talks sense?		

3.3

You're making it up!

LEVEL
Advanced

ACTIVITY TYPE
Definitions game

MATERIALS
One set of the 12 collocation + definition slips (Part A of the worksheet), cut up for group work, and a further copy (*not* cut up) for each student for reference after the activity
One copy of the gap fill (Part B) for each student.

TARGET COLLOCATIONS
apologise profusely,
ask a favour,
backhanded compliment,
drop a hint,
exchange pleasantries,
feeble excuse,
fish for compliments,
hazard a guess,
pay *someone* a compliment,
pick a fight,
rash promise,
sweeping generalisation,
tentative suggestion,
wild accusation

TIME
45 minutes

Warmer
1   Tell the class that the lesson will focus on collocations relating to communication.
2   Write *pay someone a* _ _ _ _ _ _ _ _ _ on the board.
3   Put students in two teams and give each team a starting score of five points. Ask each team to take it in turns to guess a letter. For each letter they guess correctly they get one point; for each letter they guess incorrectly they lose one point.
4   When the whole word (compliment) has been guessed, elicit/explain the meaning of the collocation.
5   Repeat the process with *ask a* _ _ _ _ _ _ (favour).
    Leave the collocations written up on the board for reference later in the lesson.

Input
1   Tell students that they are now going to play a definitions game with other collocations relating to communication.
2   Put students in groups and share out all the 'collocation + definition' slips (Part A of the worksheet), between the groups. Each slip should be given out only once in the class.
3   Ask each group to write two false definitions for each collocation they have. Explain that when they have finished they will ask the other groups to guess which definition is the correct one, so at least one of their false definitions should sound possible.
4   When they have finished, ask a spokesperson from each team in turn to write the collocation on the board and read out the three definitions. The rest of the class then vote for the definition they think is the real one.
5   The team that manages to deceive the highest number of people wins.
6   Give each student a copy of Part A – not cut up into slips, for reference.

Practice
1   Put students in pairs. Give each pair a copy of the gap fill sentences (Part B of the worksheet) and have them complete them with the collocations from the warmer and Part A in the correct form.

> **Answer key**
> **1** sweeping generalisations   **2** rash promise   **3** feeble excuse   **4** pick a fight
> **5** wild accusation   **6** exchanged pleasantries   **7** compliment paid   **8** fishing for compliments   **9** backhanded compliment   **10** dropping hints   **11** hazard a guess
> **12** ask a favour   **13** apologised profusely   **14** tentative suggestion

Follow-up
Leave the collocations up on the board. Ask students in pairs to think of ways of saying the opposite of these collocations. Note that these opposites will not always be collocations themselves, but that the exercise should lead to a productive discussion of vocabulary (e.g. *apologise profusely* – opposite: make a half-hearted apology; *a feeble excuse* – opposite: a good/valid/plausible excuse).

> **Sample answers**
> apologise profusely – opposite: make a half-hearted apology
> ask someone a favour – opposite: offer to do something for someone
> a backhanded compliment – opposite: the ultimate compliment
> drop a hint about something – opposite: ask outright
> a feeble excuse – opposite: a good/valid/plausible excuse
> pay someone a compliment – opposite: insult someone, criticise someone
> a rash promise – opposite: a promise made after careful consideration
> a sweeping generalisation – opposite: a specific point
> a tentative suggestion – opposite: a concrete/firm plan
> a wild accusation – opposite: an accusation based on evidence

● See page 125–6 for the best games from the CD-ROM to play after this unit.

A Collocation + definition slips

a wild accusation	an accusation which is not based on facts and is probably wrong
a backhanded compliment	a remark that seems to praise someone but also criticises them
a sweeping generalisation	a statement that is not fair because it is very general and not based on particular facts
pick a fight	to try to start an argument with someone
exchange pleasantries	to talk briefly and politely with someone, saying things that are not really very important
a feeble excuse	a weak excuse that is not good enough
fish for compliments	to try to make someone praise you
a rash promise	a promise that is made too quickly and has not been thought about carefully
drop a hint	to tell someone something in a way that is not direct
hazard a guess	to risk guessing something
apologise profusely	to apologise a lot
a tentative suggestion	a suggestion that you are not certain about

B Use the collocations you have learned to complete these gap fill sentences.

1 He made some .... about men and women – all the usual stereotypes.

2 I had started to regret my .... to cook for everyone.

3 I explained that I wouldn't be coming to the party because I had to pack for my holiday but he clearly thought it was a ....

4 Don't take any notice of him. He was just trying to .... a .... – he loves arguing.

5 You can't go making a .... like that with no evidence for what you are claiming.

6 We .... but I didn't get to talk to him properly.

7 Thank you! That's the nicest .... anyone has ever .... me!

8 I'm not .... so you don't need to contradict me – I genuinely don't think I'm a very good manager.

9 She said the dress made me look slim, which is a .... when you think about it.

10 She keeps .... about wanting a piece of jewellery for her birthday.

11 If I were to .... a .... I'd say she's about 45.

12 Actually, I've called to .... you a .... Could I possibly borrow your bike this weekend?

13 When she realised her mistake she ....

14 Could I just make a .... that we make these meetings a little shorter?

4.1

Who am I?

LEVEL
Elementary /
Pre-intermediate

ACTIVITY TYPE
Board game

MATERIALS
One copy of the
picture board from
the worksheet for
each student

**TARGET
COLLOCATIONS**
bald head,
big nose,
curly hair,
dark hair,
dark skin,
fair hair,
fair skin,
have a beard,
have a moustache,
long hair,
short hair,
straight hair,
wear a hat,
wear glasses

TIME
40–50 minutes

Warmer

1 Tell your students to look at the person they are sitting next to and write three sentences describing their appearance, e.g. *Rudi has dark hair. He has blue eyes. He is wearing black trousers.*

2 Ask some of the students to read their sentences to the class.

Input

1 Give out a copy of the worksheet picture board to each student. Divide the class into two groups and explain that you are going to have a competition to see which group can be the first to find someone matching your description. The first team to shout out a correct answer gets a point. For example, if you say, *Find someone who wears glasses*, they could shout out *Pavel* or *Max*.

2 Make sure you have covered all the target collocations, and write them on the board as you go along.

Practice

1 Explain that you are going to play a game called *Who am I?*

2 Demonstrate the game by choosing a character from the board, but do not tell the class who it is. Explain that you are now one of the characters from the board and the students have to ask you questions to try to identify who you are, e.g. *Do you have short hair?*, *Do you wear glasses?* etc. Continue until the students have identified which character you are from the board.

3 Put students in pairs to play the game. They take it in turns to ask one question each. By a process of elimination, they work out who their opponent's character is, and the first one to guess correctly is the winner. Explain that they should not guess the character until they are absolutely certain. (If they guess incorrectly, the other student wins.)

4 The game can be played several times and with different partners.

Follow-up

1 Ask each student to think of a famous person from their country. They should write five sentences describing their appearance.

2 Have each student read out their description for the rest of the class to guess who their person is.

See page 125–6 for the best games from the CD-ROM to play after this unit.

Picture board

Marcel	Maria	Pavel	Hannah	Max
Wolfgang	Ollie	Peter	Rosa	Annie
Isabella	Eva	Boris	Laura	Kazuo
Julio	Sebastian	Sara	Zoe	Clara

4.2

Wanted!

LEVEL
Intermediate

ACTIVITY TYPE
Writing descriptions

MATERIALS
One copy of the texts and gap fill sentences (Part A of the worksheet) for each student
One copy of the pictures (Part B) for each pair.

TARGET COLLOCATIONS
bald patch,
broad shoulders,
broken teeth,
bushy eyebrows,
cheeky grin,
chubby cheeks,
full lips,
heavy build,
lined face,
long eyelashes,
long nose,
narrow shoulders,
pointed chin,
shoulder-length hair,
slim build

TIME
45 minutes

Warmer

Review words for parts of the face by pointing and eliciting.

Input

1 Put students in pairs. Give each pair a copy of the three texts (Part A of the worksheet), and have them work together to fill the gaps.

2 Give out the remaining copies of the text so that each student has a copy. Check answers and make sure everyone understands the collocations.

> **Answer key**
> 1 long, chubby, cheeky, heavy, broad
> 2 long, broken, bald, slim, narrow
> 3 shoulder-length, bushy, full, pointed, lined

Practice

1 Ask the students what the texts are (descriptions of crime suspects) and explain that they are now going to look at a police line-up of nine suspects.

2 Put students in new pairs and give each pair a copy of the pictures (Part B of the worksheet). Have them look at the pictures and choose the criminal to match each text (from Part A).

3 Check answers.

> **Answer key**
> **text 1**: picture 9   **text 2**: picture 6   **text 3**: picture 2

Follow-up

1 Have each pair choose one of the six remaining pictures in Part B and them write their own description, using the collocations they have learned.

2 When they have done this, each pair should swap their description with the pair next to them and try to guess which picture the other pair has written about.

Variation

1 If your class enjoy drawing, have each pair invent their own criminal. They should write a short description of their criminal, using at least four of the collocations they have learned, and draw a picture of them on a separate A4 sheet of paper.

2 Collect in the pictures and the descriptions. Pin the pictures to the wall. Shuffle the descriptions and hand them out, making sure nobody gets their own back.

3 Have each pair match the description they have to one of the pictures on the wall.

⦿ See page 125–6 for the best games from the CD-ROM to play after this unit.

A Read each text and complete the gaps.

1 CCTV footage shows a short man with a hood pulled over his head. However, it is still possible to make out a .... nose, ... cheeks and a .... grin as he grabs the cash. He is thought to be around 20, of .... build and with .... shoulders.

| heavy | long | cheeky | chubby | broad |

2 A female witness described how she noticed the thief's particularly .... eyelashes. 'I thought he was really handsome,' she said, 'until he started shouting and I could see his .... teeth. And when he turned round, I could see he had a .... patch too.' The man is thought to be in his late thirties, of .... build and with .... shoulders.

| bald | slim | broken | narrow | long |

3 Police say the man seen running from the crime scene was about 6 feet tall, wearing a torn leather jacket. He had .... hair and very .... eyebrows. He had .... lips and a particularly .... chin. He is thought to be in his sixties or seventies as he has a very .... face.

| pointed | shoulder-length | lined | full | bushy |

B

4.3

Find a friend

LEVEL
Advanced

ACTIVITY TYPE
Reading
Discussion
Writing

MATERIALS
One copy of the
worksheet for each
student
4 pieces of paper to
write on for each
pair
Dictionaries

**TARGET
COLLOCATIONS**
boundless energy,
deeply religious,
downright rude,
good listener,
good sense of humour,
highly opinionated,
impeccable manners,
infectious laugh,
keen interest,
of average intelligence,
outgoing personality,
painfully shy,
physically fit,
ready wit,
show consideration,
strong personality

TIME
45 minutes – 1 hour

Warmer

Lead a classroom discussion about what qualities people look for in a friend.

Input

1   Put students in pairs. Give each student a copy of the worksheet. Have them sort the collocations into three columns according to whether they are *positive*, *negative* or *neutral*. Allow for disagreement within the pair as the answers depend on students' own personalities (e.g. impeccable manners may be positive to some, negative to others).

2   Allow students access to dictionaries to check the meanings.

3   Conduct whole-class feedback, asking students to explain their choices. Check that students understand the meanings of the collocations.

Practice

1   Put students in new pairs. Refer them to the *Friends* task on the worksheet. Explain that the eight people are all looking for new friends.

2   Have each pair match the people in the box with one of the speakers below. They should write a short sentence, explaining why they have done that, but also what the problems might be.

3   Have each pair work with another pair to discuss their answers.

4   Conduct feedback. Ask each pair to report back any disagreements they had.

Follow-up

1   Have each student choose one of the people on the worksheet to write an ideal friend profile for.

2   When they have finished, have each student swap their profile with another student. They should read the profile, and try and identify which person it was written for.

● See page 125–6 for the best games from the CD-ROM to play after this unit.

Collocations

Decide if the collocations below are positive (✓), negative (✗) or neutral(–).

outgoing personality	deeply religious	show consideration	downright rude
boundless energy	physically fit	good sense of humour	painfully shy good listener
strong personality	highly opinionated	infectious laugh	impeccable manners
of average intelligence	ready wit		

Which of the speakers below would make good friends for Thomas, Gisèle, Elisabeth and Ivan?

Thomas: I am a successful academic at a leading university. I am looking for someone with an **outgoing personality** who I can go to social events with. I have a **keen interest** in architecture, and I enjoy going to restaurants.

Gisèle: I am a **deeply religious** person, and although I do not expect all my friends to believe, they must be thoughtful and **show consideration** for my views. I have met too many people who have been **downright rude** about my faith.

Elisabeth: I would like to meet some friends to go walking with. Preferably people with **boundless energy** since I love climbing mountains! I am slim and **physically fit**, though not at all intellectual. I can't sit still long enough to read a book!

Ivan: I'd like to go to more gigs, but I'm fed up with going alone. I love jazz, but I enjoy any music as long as it's good. I'm looking for people with **a good sense of humour**. I love swimming and judo and I collect stamps from all over the world.

Ben: I've decided that I need to get fit. I'm looking for friends who want to do anything active – waterskiing, training for a marathon, or even climbing Everest! I am of average intelligence, but I'd like to think I have a ready wit and I'm always keen to learn something new.

Peter: I'm looking for someone to go travelling with. I find it difficult to make friends, because I've always been painfully shy, but the friends I do have say that I am very loyal and sensitive and I'm definitely a good listener. I love music, especially hip hop and house.

Christa: I like to make friends with interesting, eccentric people. I like my friends to have a strong personality and to be highly opinionated so that we can have good discussions! I love good food, and having fun. People say I have an infectious laugh, and I certainly enjoy telling jokes.

Anna: I like my friends to have impeccable manners. For instance, I think you should always write a note to thank someone who has cooked a meal for you. I enjoy playing hockey and squash, and I go to the gym at least three times a week. I am a scientist, and I have actually written a book about my hero, Charles Darwin.

5.1

Feelings

LEVEL
Elementary /
Pre-intermediate

ACTIVITY TYPE
Matching sentences
Sentence
completion

MATERIALS
One copy of the
emoticons (Part A of
the worksheet) for
each group of three
or four students
One copy of the
pictures and
captions (Part B) for
each student
One copy of the mix
and match sentence
halves (Part C) for
each student
One set of nine
blank slips of paper
for each pair

**TARGET
COLLOCATIONS**
feel angry
feel bored
feel excited
feel happy
feel lonely
feel pleased
feel sad
feel upset
make *someone* angry
make *someone* cry
make *someone* happy
make *someone* laugh
make *someone* sad
make *someone* smile

TIME
45 minutes

Warmer

1 Put students in groups of three or four. Give each group a copy of the emoticons (Part A of the worksheet).

2 Give the groups three minutes to decide what emotions the emoticon faces are showing.

3 Conduct feedback, discussing the different possible answers below as appropriate.

> **Answer key**
> 1 happy 2 sad 3 angry 4 crying 5 laughing 6 bored

Input

1 Put students in pairs. Give each pair a copy of the pictures and captions (Part B of the worksheet). Ask them to match the pictures to the correct captions.

2 Give out the remaining copies of Part B so that each student has a copy.

3 Check answers.

> **Answer key**
> 1 b 2 e 3 g 4 a 5 h 6 i 7 c 8 d 9 f

Practice

1 Keep the students in their pairs. Give each pair a set of broken sentences to match.

2 Give out the remaining copies of Part C so that each student has a copy.

3 Check answers. Remember some students may have made other sentences which are also possible.

> **Possible answers**
> 1 I feel happy when I am with my friends.
> 2 I feel bored when I have nothing to do.
> 3 Saying goodbye for a long time makes me sad.
> 4 I feel lonely when I am far away from home.
> 5 My friend Paolo is very funny – he makes me laugh.
> 6 Sunshine makes me happy.
> 7 I feel excited before I go on holiday.
> 8 Sad films make me cry.
> 9 When my football team play badly, it makes me angry.

Follow-up

1 Ask students to put the sentence halves that do not contain a collocation to one side.

2 Keep the students in their pairs and give each pair a set of blank slips of paper. Ask them to complete the sentences from the practice activity with a different beginning or ending of their own choice.

3 Ask each pair to work with another pair. Each pair should swap their papers with the other pair and try to match the two halves of the sentences. Some beginnings and endings may be interchangeable so make sure that pairs accept any logical matches.

See page 125–6 for the best games from the CD-ROM to play after this unit.

A How do they feel?

1   2   3   4   5   6

B

Match the captions to the pictures.

a Julio **made** him **laugh**.

b She **made** her mother very **happy**.

c For the first time in weeks, he **felt happy**.

d It was Anna's birthday the next day and she was **feeling** very **excited**.

e His teacher **made** him **cry**.

f Paolo said something that **made** him **angry**.

g He **felt** so **bored** during maths lessons.

h She **felt** too **sad/upset** to talk.

i Sara **felt lonely** when she wasn't with her family.

C Match the sentence halves.

1 I **feel happy** when

2 I **feel bored** when

3 Saying goodbye for a long time

4 I **feel lonely** when

5 My friend Paolo is very funny – he

6 Sunshine

7 I **feel excited** before

8 Sad films

9 When my football team play badly, it

I have nothing to do.

I am far away from home.

makes me **happy**.

makes me **angry**.

I go on holiday.

I am with my friends.

make me **cry**.

makes me **laugh**.

makes me **sad**.

5.2

Consequences

LEVEL
Intermediate

ACTIVITY TYPE
Gap fill sentences
Playing Consequences

MATERIALS
One copy of the
sentences (Part A of
the worksheet) for
each student
One Consequence
sheet (Part B) for
each student

**TARGET
COLLOCATIONS**
be absolutely
delighted,
be in a bad mood,
be in a good mood,
be wildly excited,
be worried sick,
burst into tears,
burst out laughing,
drive *someone* crazy,
drive *someone* mad,
get a real buzz,
hurt *someone's*
feelings,
jump for joy,
lose your temper

TIME
45 minutes – 1 hour

Warmer

1   Elicit/teach the terms *good mood* and *bad mood*.
2   Ask students what things put them in a good mood and what things put them in a bad mood.

Input

1   Put student in pairs. Give each pair a copy of the sentences (Part A of the worksheet) and ask them to fill the gaps in the sentences using the words in the box.
2   Give out the remaining copies of Part A so that each student has a copy.
3   Check answers.

> **Answer key**
> **1** temper   **2** feelings   **3** sick   **4** buzz   **5** mad/crazy   **6** laughing   **7** mood
> **8** tears   **9** delighted   **10** excited   **11** bad   **12** joy

Practice

1   Put students in small groups (of 4–6). Explain that you are going to play a game called *Consequences*. (Explain that a consequence is something that happens as a result of an action.)
2   Give every member of each group the same Consequence card (from Part B of the worksheet) and ask them to look at the four half-sentences. Explain that each person in the group must copy the first half-sentence on to a piece of paper, and then complete the sentence in an imaginative or funny way. Then each person should fold their sentence over so it cannot be seen (demonstrate this part).
3   Explain that they must then pass their paper on to the person on their right, who in turn will copy out and complete the second half-sentence, fold the paper as before and pass it on as before.
4   When all four half-sentences on the cards have been completed, each student should unfold their paper and read out what is written.
5   Ask students to swap Consequences cards with another group and play the game again.

Follow-up

1   Give each group of four one of the Consequences cards (Part B) that they did not see in the Practice.
2   Have each group write an extended story based on the sentence beginnings on their Consequences cards, but expanding much more on them than in the previous activity, and adding any extra collocations that they like.
3   Display the stories around the room for other students to read.

● See page 125–6 for the best games from the CD-ROM to play after this unit.

A Fill in the gaps in the sentences using the words in the box.

excited	bad	mad	laughing	joy	temper	feelings	mood	sick	buzz	tears	delighted

1　His daughter's behaviour made him **lose his** .... and he punched the door.

2　Jane **hurt** Paolo's .... by telling him he looked fat.

3　Alex was two hours late home from school so his mother was **worried** .... about him.

4　Jan loves extreme sports – he **gets a real** .... out of surfing and snowboarding.

5　Carlo was **driving** me .... with his terrible singing.

6　I **burst out** .... when I saw how funny he looked.

7　I **was in a good** .... because it was my birthday.

8　Charles began shouting at her and she immediately **burst into** ....

9　Tiane was **absolutely** .... with the birthday present her boyfriend gave her.

10　The children were **wildly** .... about their trip to the zoo the next day.

11　I overslept this morning and I've **been in a** .... **mood** for the rest of the day.

12　I **jumped for** .... when I found out that I had won the competition.

✂ -

B Consequences cards

✂ - ✂ -

1　Tom was worried sick because …

_____

2　The problem was driving him crazy and he …

_____

3　Finally, he lost his temper and …

_____

4　And the consequence for Tom was …

1　Kurt was in a bad mood because …

_____

2　That morning he had hurt his wife's feelings by telling her …

_____

3　She had burst into tears and …

_____

4　And the consequence for Kurt and his wife was …

✂ -

1　Sylvie was in a good mood because …

_____

2　She was absolutely delighted because her mother had promised …

_____

3　This made her burst out laughing and …

_____

4　And the consequence for Sylvie was …

1　Mario gets a real buzz out of …

_____

2　So he was wildly excited about …

_____

3　He jumped for joy when he heard …

_____

4　And the consequence for Mario was …

5.3

Dominoes

LEVEL
Advanced

ACTIVITY TYPE
Dominoes
Text substitution

MATERIALS
One copy of the
word forks (Part A of
the Worksheet) for
each student
One copy of the
sentences (Part B) for
each pair of students
One set of dominoes
(Part C of the
worksheet) cut up for
each group of three
or four students
Advanced learner
dictionaries

**TARGET
COLLOCATIONS**
bitterly/deeply
disappointed,
blissfully happy,
bored stiff,
bored out of your mind,
deeply distressed,
deeply offended,
deeply/profoundly
depressed,
deeply/profoundly
shocked,
highly amused,
highly irritated,
intensely irritated,
insanely jealous,
mildly amused,
mildly depressed,
mildly irritated,
madly in love,
profoundly grateful

TIME
45 minutes

Warmer

1 Put students in pairs. Give each pair a copy of the collocations (Part A of the worksheet) describing emotions and decide whether they are positive or negative emotions.

2 Conduct whole-class feedback.

Input

1 Give out the remaining copies of Part A so each student has a copy and explain that this shows which adverbs collocate with which adjectives.

2 Ask students to work individually to try to memorise the collocations.

3 After one minute lead a discussion about what memory techniques they used to remember the collocations.

4 Give the students a further minute to try to memorise the collocations, perhaps using one of the other memory techniques that was discussed.

Practice

1 Put students in pairs and give each pair a copy of the sentences (Part B of the worksheet). Explain that they should try to replace the word *very* or *quite* in each sentence with a more interesting adverb. They should do this from memory, recalling the combinations they looked at in the Input (Part A).

2 Check answers.

> **Answer key**
> **1** bitterly/deeply **2** highly **3** blissfully **4** intensely **5** (bored) stiff/(bored) out of my mind **6** mildly **7** mildly **8** deeply **9** deeply/profoundly **10** deeply
> **11** profoundly **12** deeply/profoundly **13** insanely **14** madly

Follow-up

1 Give each group of three or four students a copy of the dominoes (you may need to enlarge these on the photocopier). Ask the students to divide up the dominoes equally between them.

2 Explain that they must take it in turns to put down a domino that collocates with the word that it is placed next to.

3 The students work as a team. If any player cannot go, the other students must check that student's dominoes and see if they can make any suggestions. Stress that this is a team activity.

4 If a player really cannot go, the next player takes a turn.

5 All teams work together until they have put down as many of the dominoes as possible.

● See page 125–6 for the best games from the CD-ROM to play after this unit.

A Word forks

Can you memorise the collocations?

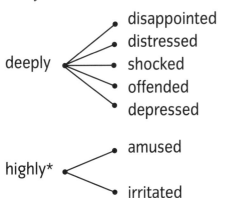

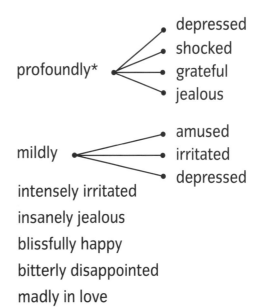

intensely irritated

insanely jealous

blissfully happy

bitterly disappointed

madly in love

bored stiff# / out of your mind

* formal   #informal

✂---

B Replace the word 'very' or 'quite' in each sentence with a more interesting adverb.

1   She was *very* **disappointed** when she failed.

2   I was *very* **amused** by his comments.

3   We had a *very* **happy** marriage.

4   I am *very* **irritated** by her attitude.

5   I'm *very* **bored** at work.

6   I was *quite* **amused** by the film.

7   I suppose I was *quite* **irritated** by what she said.

8   I saw her after the news and she was *very* **distressed**.

9   We were both *very* **shocked** by her death.

10 He was evidently *very* **offended** by the criticism.

11 We are *very* **grateful** for your help.

12 He had been *very* **depressed** for many months.

13 He is *very* **jealous** of her ex-boyfriend.

14 We were both young and *very* **in love**.

✂---

C Dominoes

happy	highly	amused	bitterly
depressed	blissfully	disappointed	insanely
stiff	profoundly	shocked	mildly
out of your mind	mildly	bored	deeply
irritated	deeply	offended	intensely
distressed	deeply	bored	profoundly
amused	intensely	depressed	madly
irritated	mildly	in love	profoundly
grateful	profoundly	jealous	deeply
shocked	deeply	disappointed	insanely

6.1

A life of learning

LEVEL
Elementary /
Pre-intermediate

ACTIVITY TYPE
Information gap

MATERIALS
One copy of the
story and gap fill
nouns (Part A of the
worksheet) for each
pair
A copy of one of the
character grids (Part
B) for each pair

**TARGET
COLLOCATIONS**
do a course,
do your homework,
go to college,
go to school,
go to university,
leave school,
pass/fail an exam,
start school,
take an exam,
write an essay

TIME
45 – 50 minutes

Warmer

1   Ask students at what age they started school and how many schools they went / have been to?

2   Use these questions to elicit/teach *primary school, secondary school, college, university*.

Input

1   Put students in pairs. Give each pair a copy of the gap fill paragraph, *Simon's story* (Part A of the worksheet). Ask them to use the words in the collocations box to fill in the gaps.

> **Answer key**
>
> **1** started   **2** went to   **3** take   **4** writing   **5** failed   **6** leave   **7** go to
> **8** do   **9** do   **10** passed

2   Refer students to the gap fills (1–6) under the text and ask them to complete them with verbs from the text in their infinitive form.

3   Check answers.

> **Answer key**
>
> **1** start/go to/leave school   **2** do your homework   **3** write an essay
> **4** do/fail/pass an exam   **5** go to university   **6** do a course

Practice

1   Give half the class Grid 1, and half the class Grid 2. Put each student in a pair with another student who has the same grid.

2   Using the facts they have been given, ask the pairs to write a story similar to Simon's story about their own character, using Simon's story as a model. Encourage stronger students to add extra details, such as whether or not their character enjoyed school, or what they studied at college.

3   Re-group the students into new pairs so that each student is working with someone who has a different grid to them.

4   Ask the pairs to take it in turns to read their stories out loud. As one student reads aloud, the other student should fill in the missing details on their grid.

Follow-up

1   Put students into pairs. Ask each pair to tell each other about their own education. The students should take notes on what their partner says, and ask questions if they want to.

2   Then everyone finds a new partner and tells them about the education of their previous partner. Again, everyone should take notes.

3   Then, each person finds the student they were told about, and tells them what they have learned. That person tells them whether it is correct or not.

See page 125–6 for the best games from the CD-ROM to play after this unit.

A Complete the text using words from the box.

| started | passed | do | went to | writing | failed | take | go to | leave | do |

Simon's story

"I (1) .... school at the age of five. I (2) .... school in our village. When I was eleven, I moved to the secondary school in the nearest town, and went there every day on the bus. I was a terrible pupil. I never remembered to (3) .... my homework into school and I hated (4) .... essays. I (5) .... most of my exams. At sixteen, I was glad to (6) .... school. I certainly did not want to (7) .... university. But a few years ago, my friend and I decided to (8) .... a course in furniture making in the evenings. I loved it and even decided to (9) .... the exam at the end of the course. I (10) .... the exam, and now I have a good job as a furniture maker."

Now fill the gaps below with verbs from the text in their infinitive form.

1 .... / .... / .... school
2 .... your homework
3 .... an essay

4 .... / .... / .... an exam
5 .... university
6 .... a course

✁- -

B Grid 1

	Ferdi	Astrid
started school	5	
went to primary school	city	
went to secondary school	11	
good pupil	yes	
did homework	always	
wrote good essays	yes	
passed exams	yes, all	
left school	18	
went to university	yes	
did another course	yes, Japanese	

Grid 2

	Ferdi	Astrid
started school		7
went to primary school		village
went to secondary school		12
good pupil		no
did homework		never
wrote good essays		no
passed exams		a few
left school		16
went to university		no
did another course		yes, hairdressing

6.2

Which school?

LEVEL
Intermediate

ACTIVITY TYPE
Reading
Discussion
Writing

MATERIALS
One copy of the worksheet for each student

TARGET COLLOCATIONS
carry out experiments,
complete your studies,
continue your studies,
do project work,
enrol on a course,
get bored,
good sports facilities,
hand in your work,
learn *something* by heart,
natural talent,
pay attention,
play truant,
quick learner

TIME
45 minutes – 1 hour

Warmer

1   Explain that you are going to be talking about schools and learning.

2   Ask each student to think about their own secondary school and write down two things they like/liked about it and two things they don't/didn't like.

3   Ask some of the students to read their sentences to the class.

Input

1   Put the students in pairs. Give each pair a copy of the worksheet. Explain that the three parents are looking for schools for their teenage children.

2   Ask each pair to read about the teenagers and, for each text, find the collocations that match the definitions.

> **Answer key**
>
> **Text 1:**   **1** quick learner   **2** get bored   **3** carry out experiments
> **4** do project work   **5** continue (your) studies
>
> **Text 2:**   **1** pay attention   **2** natural talent   **3** good sports facilities
> **4** enrol (on a course)
>
> **Text 3:**   **1** play truant   **2** learn something by heart   **3** hand in (your) work
> **4** Complete (your) studies

Practice

1   Have students work individually. Ask them to read the two school prospectuses.

2   Put the students in pairs and ask them to discuss which school each teenager should go to. Ask them to write three or four sentences giving reasons and potential problems.

3   Check answers.

Follow-up

1   Put students in groups of three or four, and ask them to write a prospectus for their ideal school. They should try to use some of the collocations they have learned.

2   Pin the prospectuses to the wall and ask everyone to look at them and decide which school they'd like to go to.

See page 125–6 for the best games from the CD-ROM to play after this unit.

A

In text 1 below, find collocations that mean:

1   someone who finds it easy to learn new things fast: a ....
2   to lose interest in something: to ....
3   to do tests in a science lab: to ....
4   to do studies of a particular subject for a period of time: to ....
5   to carry on studying after school: to .... your ....

> My daughter Kim is a very quick learner and gets bored if the work is too easy. She loves science, and enjoys carrying out experiments. We feel that a good education is when pupils do project work and learn things for themselves. It is not just about giving information. Young minds should be allowed to think for themselves! Kim hopes to continue her studies at university, and her ambition is to become an astronaut.

In text 2 below, find collocations that mean:

1   to concentrate on what you are doing: to ....
2   an ability you are born with: ....
3   sports equipment, playing fields, etc: ....
4   to arrange to do a course: to ....

> We are looking for a friendly and caring school for our son Yuri. He is a pleasant and polite boy, but he finds it difficult to pay attention in class. The problem is that he is always dreaming about becoming a famous footballer, so he forgets about everything else. He does have a natural talent for sport, so it is important that we choose a school that has good sports facilities. Yuri has struggled with his exams, but he has recently enrolled on a course to improve his maths and English.

In text 3 below, find collocations that mean:

1   to stay away from school when you should be there: to ....
2   to learn facts so that you can remember them: to ....
3   to give your work to a teacher: to .... your ....
4   to finish the course you are doing: to .... your ....

> The main thing we are looking for is a school that has good discipline! Our daughter Lily is quite wild, and has recently begun to play truant, going back home in the morning after we have gone to work. She needs a good, old-fashioned education, with plenty of learning by heart. If she does not hand in her work on time, we expect her to be punished. As you can probably tell, we are desperate. If she does not complete her studies, she will ruin her life.

B

Oak Green School

At Oak Green School, our motto is 'Work for Success'. We use traditional teaching methods to achieve the highest examination results in the county. Thanks to the generosity of our former pupils, the school now has an indoor swimming pool, a modern IT centre, and an outstanding library. We expect our pupils to work hard and develop a mature approach to learning. In return, they receive a first-class education – we aim to produce the leaders of the future. Our pupils wear their uniforms with pride.

Valley View School

At Valley View, we treat each pupil as an individual. We encourage all talents – academic, sporting and musical. We believe that pupils learn best by discovery. There is an emphasis on practical experiments, and our lessons are designed to support pupils in their own learning, at their own speed. Facilities in the school include extensive playing fields and a modern gym, a theatre and our own recording studios.

6.3

LEVEL
Advanced

ACTIVITY TYPE
Reading
Ordering sentences
Discussion

MATERIALS
One copy of the collocations and their paraphrases (Part A of the worksheet) for each pair
One copy of the sentences (part B), cut up in slips and shuffled

TARGET COLLOCATIONS
attend lectures,
background reading,
continuous assessment,
drop out of university,
formal qualifications,
gifted children,
give feedback,
marked improvement,
mixed-ability class,
raise standards,
room for improvement,
vocational training,
your attention wanders

TIME
40–50 minutes

A good education

Warmer

Put students in pairs. Have them tell each other something about their own education, and what they liked and did not like about it. Ask one or two students to tell the class what their partner said.

Input

1   Give out Part A of the worksheet to each pair, and ask them to match the collocations to the paraphrases.

2   Give out the remaining copies of Part A so that each student has a copy. Check answers.

> **Answer key**
> **1** c **2** f **3** d **4** b **5** e **6** j **7** k **8** a **9** l **10** h **11** m
> **12** g **13** i

Practice

1   Keep the students in their pairs. Give each pair a copy of the cut-up sentences (Part B).

2   Explain that they have to use the sentences to make two paragraphs on separate topics.

3   Check answers by asking two students to read out a paragraph each.

4   Then, put the students into new pairs. Ask each pair to write two paragraphs expressing the opposite of the paragraphs they have. Explain that they will not be able to write an exact opposite for each sentence, but the overall sense of the text should be the opposite of the paragraphs they have. If necessary, start off the first paragraph as a class, e.g *Ludo always wanted to go to university. He concentrated hard in lectures and spent hours doing background reading.*

Follow-up

Have a class discussion about the relative responsibilities of pupils, schools, teachers and parents. Try to encourage everyone to contribute. Questions you might ask to stimulate discussion include:

●   How much homework should a 5-/10-/15-year old do?

●   Is it the role of teachers or parents to teach children about life, e.g. *morals, financial responsibility, health?*

●   If a child is disruptive at school, should parents take responsibility?

●   What is the best way to persuade a child that education is important?

● See page 125–6 for the best games from the CD-ROM to play after this unit.

A Match the collocations with the definitions

a comment on the way someone did something, especially to help them improve

1 your attention wanders

2 background reading

b go to large classes to hear talks given by teachers or professors

c you start thinking about something else

3 room for improvement

d something is not as good as it could be

4 attend lectures

e leave university early (without a qualification)

5 drop out of university

f texts you read to learn more about a subject or as preparation for a course

6 formal qualifications

7 marked improvement

g lessons for teaching practical skills needed for work

8 give feedback

h classes where students of different abilities are taught together

9 raise standards

i when students' work during a course is graded and forms part of their qualifications

10 mixed-ability class

11 gifted children

j official records proving that someone has a certain skill, ability or knowledge that has been tested

12 vocational training

13 continuous assessment

k when something gets noticeably better

l to improve the quality of something

m pupils who are very talented

B

Text 1

Ludo never really wanted to go to university, but his parents insisted he should go.

Right from the beginning, his attention wandered during lectures, and he could never be bothered to do any of the background reading.

He passed his first year exams, but his tutors told him there was certainly room for improvement.

In the second year, he stopped attending lectures, and spent most of his time practising the guitar in his room.

Then, to his parents' horror, he decided to drop out of university and join a band.

He simply explained that, for him, university was a waste of time as he didn't need any formal qualifications to be a musician.

Text 2

Since the last inspectors' report, there has been a marked improvement in the standards at Valley View School.

Teachers are now regularly given feedback on their performance, and this has helped to raise standards.

In addition, the mixed-ability classes are much more efficiently organised than at the time of the last inspection.

Whereas the more gifted children had previously been largely ignored, they are now receiving challenging extension work, while classroom assistants are devoting more time to less able students.

There has been a welcome increase in vocational training, and students now have the option of continuous assessment of their work rather than end-of-year exams.

7.1

A bad day

LEVEL
Elementary /
Pre-intermediate

ACTIVITY TYPE
Matching collocations
Ordering pictures to
tell a story

MATERIALS
One copy of the
problems and the
solutions (Part A of
the worksheet) for
each pair
One copy of the six
Maria pictures (Part
B of the worksheet)
and her story (Part
D) for half the pairs
in the class
One copy of the six
Sven pictures (Part C)
and his story (Part E)
for the other pairs

**TARGET
COLLOCATIONS**
call the helpdesk,
car won't start,
computer crashes,
find your house keys,
have a headache,
late for work,
lose your house keys,
miss the train,
take a tablet,
take a taxi,
wait for the (next) train,
work/stay late (in the
office)

TIME
40–50 minutes

Warmer

Tell the students that today you are going to be talking about problems and ways of solving problems. Introduce them to the collocation *bad day* and ask them what might happen on a bad day.

Input

1   Elicit/teach the words *problem* and *solution*.

2   Put students in pairs. Give out the list of problems and solutions (Part A) to each pair, and explain that there are six problems and six solutions. Ask them to match the problems with the solutions. Explain that some problems may have several solutions, but that they have to make sure that every problem has a solution.

3   Check answers.

> **Answer key**
> Although some problems match with more than one solution, the following combinations ensure that each problem has a solution:
>
> **1** take a tablet (c)   **2** find your house keys (f)   **3** wait for the next train (a)
> **4** work late (e)   **5** call the helpdesk (b)   **6** take a taxi (d)

Practice

1   Put students into groups of four. For the first stage, students will work in pairs within their group. Give one pair in each group the set of pictures about Maria and give the other pair the set of pictures about Sven. Explain that these pictures tell the story of a bad day.

2   Ask each pair to order their pictures to make the story of Maria's or Sven's bad day.

3   Now ask the pairs to use the collocations and pictures in order to tell the story of Maria's/Sven's day.

4   Give each pair a copy of the correct story (Parts D and E of the worksheet) and ask them to check the order of their pictures, rearranging if necessary.

5   Now change the pairings in each group so that each student is working with a partner from the other pair. Each new pair should now take it in turns to tell their story to their partners, without looking at the text, and their partner should listen and put the pictures in the correct order.

Follow-up

The students think about a bad day that they have had. Ask them to take five minutes to write three or four sentences about problems they had. Ask them to get into pairs and tell each other what happened that day.

● See page 125–6 for the best games from the CD-ROM to play after this unit.

A Match the problem to a solution.

1 have a headache   a   wait for the next train
2 lose your house keys   b   call the helpdesk
3 miss the train   c   take a tablet
4 late for work   d   take a taxi
5 computer crashes   e   work late
6 car won't start   f   find your house keys

B

C

D

Maria's bad day

Last Monday Maria had a bad day. In the morning she **missed** the **train**. She had to **wait for** the next **train**, so she was an hour **late for work**. When she arrived at the office, she **had a headache**. She **took** a **tablet** with a large drink of water and turned on her computer. That evening she had to **work late** because of her late start that morning.

E

Sven's bad day

Last Monday Sven had a bad day. First his **car wouldn't start** and he had to **take a taxi** to the office. He arrived at the office and ten minutes later his **computer crashed**. He **called the helpdesk** and they came and fixed the problem. When he got home that evening, he discovered that he had **lost** his **house keys**. He looked in his pockets. He looked on the ground. The keys were not there. Then he looked in his car. There were his house keys, on the front seat.

7.2

If I were you ...

LEVEL
Intermediate

ACTIVITY TYPE
Categorising
Giving advice

MATERIALS
One copy of the sentences (Part A from the worksheet), cut up for each pair
One set of problem cards and a set of collocation cards (Part B) for each pair

TARGET COLLOCATIONS
a range of options,
a tough choice,
a wide choice,
bear in mind,
consider a possibility,
consider the options,
keep in mind,
seriously consider,
the obvious choice,
the only option,
think long and hard,
your best option

TIME
40–50 minutes

Warmer

1   Choose a language you cannot speak. Tell the students that you want to learn that language really well. Ask them what you should do.

2   When they have made suggestions, ask them what they were doing when they suggested, for example, living in the country where the language is spoken. Elicit that they were *giving advice* and write the collocation on the board.

Input

1   Divide the class into pairs and give each pair a copy of the sentences (Part A of the worksheet). Explain that the sentences represent advice given by two professionals on two different subjects. Their job is to sort the sentences into two piles, one for each subject, and say which professional was advising in each case.

2   Check answers.

> **Answer key**
>
> **An estate agent advising ...**
>
> The **obvious choice** ..., **Bear in mind** that ..., There's **a wide choice of options** ..., Have you **considered** the **possibility** of ..., It sounds like the **best option** for you ..., It's a **tough choice** ...
>
> **A careers guidance officer advising ...**
>
> **Think long and hard** about ..., Have you **considered** other **options**, such as ..., your **only option** is to ..., a whole **range of options** ..., **Keep in mind** that ..., If I were you I would **seriously consider** ...

Practice

1   Now tell your students that they are going to take it in turns in pairs to give advice and take advice from each other. Divide the class into pairs and give each student a problem card from Part B of the work sheet. (You will need to duplicate these with a bigger class.)

2   Give each pair a set of collocation cards and a set of problem cards. Each pair should put the two sets of cards face down on the table.

3   Explain that the students are going to take it in turn to ask for and give advice. Student A picks up a problem card and explains their problem to their partner. Their partner (student B) now picks up a collocation card and gives student A a piece of advice using the collocation on the card (the advice can be as sensible or as silly as he/she likes).

4   The pairs continue to take turns asking for and giving advice.

Follow-up

1   Ask the students to imagine a problem and to write it at the top of a piece of A4 paper. Fold the papers and put them anonymously into a hat.

2   Ask the students to take a paper out of the hat and, using one or two collocations that they have learned in this lesson, write a piece of advice to address the problem on the paper. Ask the students to put the pieces of paper back in the hat and take out another problem.

3   Continue in this way until everyone has written three or four pieces of advice.

4   The students take the papers out of the hat (one each) and read the problems and the advice that has been offered.

> ⊙ See page 125–6 for the best games from the CD-ROM to play after this unit.

A

Sort the advice below into two groups, one for each subject. Say which professional is advising in each case.

- It sounds like the **best option** for you would be a place near the station.
- **Think long and hard** about the consequences of leaving school without any qualifications.
- If I were you I would **seriously consider** studying medicine.
- It's a **tough choice** – these are both nice properties.
- The **obvious choice**, since you use the train every day, is a property near the station.
- If you still want to go to university, your **only option** is to resit your exams.
- **Bear in mind** that houses of this quality don't come on the market every day.
- As I said before, there's a whole **range of options** for students who want to become teachers.
- There's a **wide choice of options** – for example, town houses, waterfront apartments, or perhaps bigger places away from the city centre.
- Have you **considered** other **options**, such as learning a trade?
- **Keep in mind** that it's a seven-year course.
- Have you **considered** the **possibility** of renting for a while?

B Problem cards

You want to change your hairstyle. Ask your hairdresser what style you should have.	You want to speak excellent English. Ask your director of studies how you should achieve this.	Your eyesight is getting worse. Ask your optician to advise you about glasses and contact lenses.
You want to improve the appearance of your teeth. Ask your dentist what you should do.	You want to change careers but are unsure how to do this. Ask a careers guidance officer what you should do.	You want to get fit.. Ask a personal fitness trainer in your local gym the best way to do it.
You want to buy a house/apartment in town but don't know exactly where. Ask an estate agent where to buy your property.	You need a new car. Ask a car salesperson to advise you on the best car for you.	You want a new kitchen. Ask the sales assistant in the kitchen department of a department store for advice.
You want to buy a property but don't know whether to buy a house or an apartment. Ask an estate agent to advise you.	You want to improve your tennis skills. Ask your tennis coach how you should achieve this.	You want a new bathroom. Ask the sales assistant in the bathroom department of a department store for advice.

Collocation cards

consider a possibility	keep in mind	bear in mind
a range of options	seriously consider	think long and hard
a tough choice	the only option	consider the options
a wide choice	the obvious choice	your best option

7.3

Problems at work

LEVEL
Advanced

ACTIVITY TYPE
Categorising
Making
recommendations

MATERIALS
One copy of the
pictures (Part A of
the worksheet) for
each pair
One copy of the
email (Part B) for
each student
One copy of the
problems (Part C) for
each student
Dictionaries

TARGET COLLOCATIONS
fill vacancies,
high absence rates,
inappropriate dress,
job satisfaction,
job security,
low morale,
low productivity rates,
motivate staff,
people skills,
poor performance,
poor time management,
recruit staff,
retain staff,
stress-related illness,
unprofessional attitude

TIME
45 minutes – 1 hour

Warmer

1 Put students in pairs. Give each pair a set of pictures (Part A of the worksheet) and ask them to discuss what they think the problem at work might be in each picture.

2 Conduct feedback, eliciting some of the target collocations.

3 Divide the class in half. Ask one half to imagine that they are employees of the same company, and that they are very dissatisfied with the company. Ask them to work in pairs and to list all the problems they have with the company. Ask the other half to imagine that they are the managers and they are dissatisfied with their staff. Ask them to work in pairs and list all the reasons they are dissatisfied with their staff.

4 Conduct feedback.

Input

1 Put students in pairs and give each pair a copy of the email (Part B). Tell them that the manager of a company is writing to a management consultant, explaining the problems with his/her company. (Make sure the term *management consultant* is understood.)

2 Ask the students to identify the 15 collocations which relate to problems or issues at work. Allow students to use dictionaries to check meanings.

3 Give out the remaining copies of the paragraph so that each student has a copy. Check answers and make sure that all the collocations are understood.

> **Answer key**
>
> high absence rates, stress-related illnesses, poor performance, low productivity rates, motivate staff, unprofessional attitude, inappropriate dress, poor time management, people skills, filling vacancies, recruit staff, retain staff, job satisfaction, job security, low morale

Practice

1 Write on the board the two headings *Staff recruitment and retention* and *Staff behaviour / performance*. Explain/elicit what the terms mean (*staff recruitment and retention* means employing staff and making sure that they stay with a company; *staff behaviour and performance* means how staff behave at work and how well they work).

2 Give out Part C of the worksheet. Ask the students in their pairs to identify which collocations relate to staff recruitment and retention, which to staff behaviour/ performance, and which to both and write them into the table.

3 Conduct feedback, asking the students to justify their decisions.

4 Tell the students that they are now going to be management consultants. Put the students in groups of three to four. Ask half the groups to make recommendations that address the issue of staff recruitment and retention, and the other half to make recommendations to improve staff behaviour and performance. They should base their ideas on the email from the worksheet.

5 Conduct feedback, asking different groups to present their suggestions.

Follow-up

1 Have each pair look again at Part C of the worksheet and ask them to rank the problems from a manager's perspective, from the most serious to the least serious.

2 Conduct feedback and see if you can agree on he order as a class.

● See page 125–6 for the best games from the CD-ROM to play after this unit.

A What's the problem?

B Find 15 collocations related to problems and issues at work.

Basically, there are a lot of issues in the company that are holding us back. For starters, we have unbelievably high absence rates amongst staff, many of whom complain of stress-related illnesses. Poor performance is another big issue. We have very low productivity rates, and managers are finding it harder and harder to motivate staff. Some of our staff have a completely unprofessional attitude – coming to work in inappropriate dress, showing poor time management, and demonstrating a complete lack of people skills in their dealings with clients. Another big problem for us is filling vacancies. For whatever reason, we can't recruit staff in anything like the numbers we require. Furthermore, we can't retain staff. Staff say that the lack of job satisfaction and job security has resulted in low morale.

C Work problems

Read the list of collocations below. Write them into the table under the three headings.

poor performance, high absence rates, unprofessional attitude, inappropriate dress, lack of people skills, poor time management, low productivity rates, stress-related illness, difficulty in motivating staff, difficulty in retaining staff, difficulty in recruiting staff

Staff recruitment and retention	Staff behaviour and performance	Both

8.1

Going shopping

LEVEL
Elementary /
Pre-intermediate

ACTIVITY TYPE
Picture matching
Board game
Talking about food

MATERIALS
One copy of the
board game (Part A
of the worksheet)
for each pair
One copy of the
word cards (Part B)
for each pair
A coin for each
group
A counter for each
player

**TARGET
COLLOCATIONS**
bar of chocolate,
bottle of water,
bottle of wine,
bunch of bananas,
bunch of grapes,
carton of milk,
carton of yoghurt,
jar of coffee,
jar of jam,
loaf of bread,
packet of biscuits,
packet of sweets,
tin of tomatoes

TIME
40–50 minutes

Warmer

Put students in pairs and give each pair a copy of the board game (Part A of the worksheet). Ask students to identify the items of food or drink in the pictures.

Input

1 Give a set of word cards (Part B) to each pair.

2 Ask each pair to match the cards to the pictures to make phrases such as *a carton of yoghurt*. Some words apply to more than one food or drink.

3 Check answers.

Practice

1 Put the students in groups of three. Give each group a coin, and give each student a coloured counter.

2 Tell the students that they are going to play the board game and explain the rules/ demonstrate the game:

- Students take it in turns to toss or spin the coin. If the coin lands on 'heads', they move forward one square, and if it lands on 'tails', they go forward two squares.

- When a player lands on a square, they have to ask for the item in the picture using the appropriate collocation, e.g., *Could I have a jar of coffee, please?*, The other students in the group judge whether the collocation has been used correctly. If it has, the student to the left responds (for example, *Of course, here you are*) and gives the player the word card that corresponds to the collocation. If the player has not used the collocation correctly, the player replies, *Sorry we haven't got any coffee*.

- Play continues until all the cards have been used up. The winner is the player with the most cards.

Follow-up

1 Divide the class into two groups. Ask half the class to write a shopping list of ten items they need. Ask the other half to pretend they are shopkeepers and ask them to write a list of items (unlimited number) they have in their shop. Explain that the lists can include the items studied here and/or other items. Allow one minute for the students to finish their lists.

2 Ask the shopkeeper students to stand at fixed points around the room (their shops). Ask the shopper students to visit the shops and try and buy the items on their list.

3 Continue until the first student has bought all the items on their list.

4 Conduct feedback by asking students to report back about the items they were not able to buy.

See page 125–6 for the best games from the CD-ROM to play after this unit.

A Board game

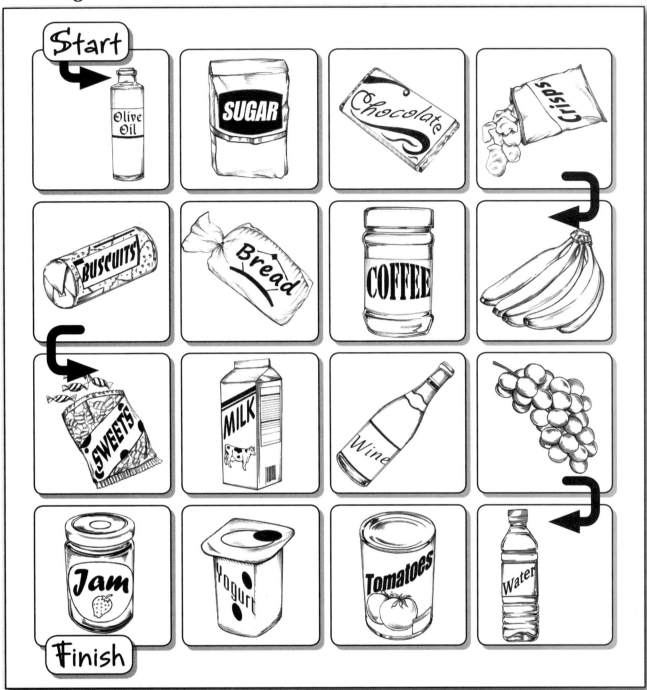

B Word cards

tin	bottle	bunch	bag
bunch	carton	jar	bottle
bar	bottle	packet	packet
carton	loaf	packet	jar

8.2

Let's cook!

LEVEL
Intermediate

ACTIVITY TYPE
Ordering texts
Mime
Describing recipes

MATERIALS
One copy of the four pictures (Part A of the worksheet) for each student
One copy of the two mixed up recipes (Part B) for each pair

TARGET COLLOCATIONS
break the eggs,
bring some water to the boil,
chop the onions,
cook the pasta,
cream the butter and sugar,
drain the pasta,
heat the oil,
melt the chocolate,
sift the flour,
skin the tomatoes,
spread the mixture,
whisk the eggs

TIME
45 minutes – 1 hour

Warmer

1 Give each student a copy of the pictures. Elicit or teach the following collocations: *slice/chop an onion, whisk eggs, sift flour, drain pasta*.

2 Put students in small groups of three or four. Give each group two minutes to make a list of other verbs that are used in cooking (e.g. *fry, stir, grate*).

3 Then ask the groups to swap their lists. Next to each verb on the list the students should write any food or drink that the verb could be done to (e.g. *fry onions, stir tea, grate cheese*).

4 Conduct feedback, writing the most useful suggestions on the board.

Input

1 Use the same groups as for the Warmer. Give each group a copy of the two recipes, cut into separate lines and mixed up.

2 Tell the class that they have two separate recipes mixed up. Explain that they should order the sentences to make two recipes and work out what the two recipes are for. Allow about ten minutes.

3 Check answers (see order on worksheet).

> **Answer key**
> Recipe one: Chocolate cake
> Recipe two: Pasta with tomato sauce

4 Ask the students to re-read the recipes and underline any verb + noun combinations like the ones from the Warmer (i.e. verb + food/drink).

5 Conduct feedback, writing the collocations on the board. Make sure that the students understand the collocations.

> **Answer key**
> cream the butter and sugar, break the eggs, melt the chocolate, whisk (the eggs), sift the flour, spread the mixture, heat the oil, chop the onions, skin the tomatoes, add the tomatoes, bring some water to the boil, cook the pasta, drain the pasta

Practice

1 Put the students in groups of three or four. Allow them 3–5 minutes to look at the recipes and try to remember them (focusing especially on the collocations).

2 Ask each group to gather up the cards in a pile and lay them face down on the table. Students take it in turns to turn over a card and mime what is written on the other side for the other students to guess. Again the focus should be on getting the collocation right, not necessarily remembering the whole sentence.

Follow-up

Ask the students to think about a dish that is often made in their own country. Give them five minutes to make notes on how to prepare it. Encourage them to use the collocations they have learned in their notes. When they have done this, ask them, in pairs, to tell their partner the name of the dish and how to prepare it. Ask one or two students to explain their partner's recipe to the class.

See page 125–6 for the best games from the CD-ROM to play after this unit.

A

1 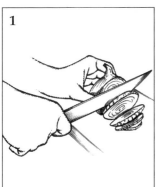	2 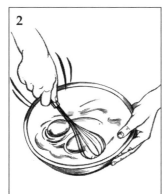	3 	4 

✁- -

B

✁- -

First, cream the butter and sugar together until light and fluffy.

- -

Break the eggs into a bowl and whisk them. Gradually stir into the butter and sugar mixture.

- -

Next, melt the chocolate in a bowl over a pan of water, and add to the mixture, stirring.

- -

Finally, sift the flour and fold into the mixture.

- -

Spread the mixture evenly in a tin and bake for 45 minutes.

- -

✁- -

First, skin the tomatoes by covering them with boiling water then carefully removing the skins.

- -

Next, chop the skinned tomatoes and then chop the onions finely.

- -

Heat the oil in a saucepan and fry the onions over a low heat for 10 minutes.

- -

Add the tomatoes to the onions, then cover the pan and simmer gently for about 20 minutes.

- -

Meanwhile, bring some water to the boil in another pan and cook the pasta according to the instructions on the packet.

- -

Drain the pasta and serve with the sauce.

- -

8.3

Restaurant reviews

LEVEL
Advanced

ACTIVITY TYPE
Jigsaw reading
Writing reviews

MATERIALS
One set of
collocations (Part A
of the worksheet)
for each student
One copy of both
restaurant reviews
(Parts B and C) for
each pair
Advanced learner
dictionaries

**TARGET
COLLOCATIONS**
à la carte menu,
creamy sauce,
crisp pastry,
efficient service,
fresh ingredients,
greasy chips,
inflated prices,
instant coffee,
limp salad,
relaxed atmosphere,
rich dessert,
seasonal vegetables,
set menu,
short-staffed,
soggy vegetables,
subtle lighting,
vegetarian option

TIME
45 minutes – 1 hour

Warmer

Explain that the lesson is going to be about food and restaurants. Ask students for the names of some restaurants they can recommend and why.

Input

1   Put students in pairs. Give each pair a copy of the collocations (Part A of the worksheet) and an advanced learner dictionary. Ask the pairs to decide whether the collocations they have made are positive, negative or neutral. Explain that there are no 'right' answers.

2   Conduct feedback, asking for opinions and checking that all the collocations are understood.

Practice

1   The students stay in their pairs. Give one student in each pair Critic 1 and the other student Critic 2. Ask students for the name and location of the restaurant (*The Three Roses, in north-west London*). Ask the students to skim read the reviews to find out whether the critic liked the restaurant. Check answers.

2   Ask the students to read the review more thoroughly and make notes on the following points: price, type of menu, main course, dessert, drinks and service. Explain that the key information for each point is not in the same order as the list, and that different pieces of information for the same point may be in different parts of the text. Allow about fifteen minutes.

3   Ask each pair to compare the notes which they have written for each point.

4   When they have both been through their texts, ask each pair to write down six to seven points where critic 1 and critic 2 have opposing views.

5   At the end, go through the differences with the whole class, reinforcing the collocations.

Answer key

	Critic 1 ...	Critic 2 ...
Price	... said that prices were reasonable.	... thought the prices were much too high.
Type of menu	... chose from the à la carte menu.	... had the set menu.
Main course	... and his/her guest really enjoyed their main courses.	... and his/her guest thought the main courses were tasteless and badly cooked.
Dessert	... thought the desserts were delicious.	... thought the desserts were heavy and too sweet.
Drinks	... had freshly ground coffee.	... was given instant coffee.
Service	... was impressed by the efficient service.	... said service was poor because the restaurant was short-staffed.
Atmosphere	... liked the relaxed atmosphere created by subtle lighting.	... said the lighting was so dim it was difficult to read the menu.

Follow-up

Ask students to write a review of a restaurant they have been to, using some of the collocations they have learned. Allow students to read each other's reviews. Encourage discussion if several students have been to one of the reviewed restaurants.

● See page 125–6 for the best games from the CD-ROM to play after this unit.

A Collocations

Decide if the collocations below are positive (✓), negative (✗) or neutral (–).

☐ à la carte menu, ☐ creamy sauce, ☐ crisp pastry, ☐ efficient service, ☐ fresh ingredients, ☐ greasy chips, ☐ inflated prices, ☐ instant coffee, ☐ limp salad, ☐ relaxed atmosphere, ☐ rich dessert, ☐ seasonal vegetables, ☐ soggy vegetables, ☐ set menu, ☐ short-staffed, ☐ subtle lighting, ☐ vegetarian option

✄ - ✄ - - - - - - - - - - - -

B Read the restaurant review below. Prepare to summarise it for your partner.

Critic 1

Imagine my excitement when I was asked to review Marcus Rose's new restaurant, The Three Roses, in north-west London. I was expecting great things from the internationally acclaimed chef and his hand-selected team – and I wasn't disappointed. This is contemporary British cuisine at its very finest, using only the **freshest ingredients**. We both chose from the **à la carte menu** and were very satisfied with our choices. My fish came in an exquisite **creamy sauce** whose richness was beautifully balanced by a generous portion of **seasonal vegetables** which were cooked to perfection. (I had a side order of sautéed potatoes too, so lightly fried that they almost tasted healthy!) My companion was similarly impressed by her onion tart – one of several enticing **vegetarian options** – a delicious combination of caramelised onions and **crisp pastry** that seemed to melt in the mouth, accompanied by a beautifully dressed green salad. Two delicious desserts followed – a light-as-air cheesecake and an extremely tasty apple tart. The freshly ground coffee that accompanied them came with two perfect home-made chocolates.

We were both very impressed by the **efficient service**. A young but well-trained staff and some very **subtle lighting** help to create a most **relaxed atmosphere** in this elegant, modern restaurant. I should also say that, for this quality of food, the prices are quite reasonable. This restaurant is a rare find indeed.

✄ - ✄ - - - - - - - - - - - -

C Read the restaurant review below. Prepare to summarise it for your partner.

Critic 2

Marcus Rose has opened a new restaurant, The Three Roses, in north-west London. I dined there yesterday evening, with high hopes for my meal. To say I was disappointed is an understatement. I'm afraid to say that this is contemporary British cuisine at its very worst – a depressing combination of over-cooked meat and **soggy vegetables** and all at outrageously **inflated prices**. We both had the **set menu** (two courses + coffee). For my main course I chose the salmon (dry and tasteless) with a side order supposedly of 'sautéed potatoes' which turned out to be nothing more than a pile of **greasy chips**. My companion was similarly unimpressed by her main course – a bland onion tart (whose pastry was so hard that when she did manage to cut into it, a piece of it flew across the restaurant and hit a fellow diner) accompanied by a rather **limp salad** (I suspect the lettuce was a few days old). To make up for the disappointment of our main courses, we both ordered **rich desserts**, a chocolate mousse for my companion and a lemon tart for me. Both were heavy and oversweet. And to cap it all, at the end of this very substandard meal, we were offered **instant coffee**! Another irritation was the lighting in the restaurant, which was so dim I could scarcely read the menu, and when I asked for help with this our waiter rudely suggested that I use my glasses. I should also add that the restaurant was so **short-staffed** yesterday evening that we struggled to get the waiter's attention. Needless to say, we didn't add a tip to the already excessively expensive bill.

9.1

LEVEL
Elementary /
Pre-intermediate

ACTIVITY TYPE
Class survey

MATERIALS
One copy of the
word forks (Part A of
the worksheet) for
each student
One copy of the
travel survey (Part B)
for each student

**TARGET
COLLOCATIONS**
catch a bus,
catch a boat,
catch a ferry,
catch a plane,
catch a train,
drive a bus
drive a car
drive a tractor
get/take a bus
get/take a coach
get/take a plane
get/take a taxi
get/take a train
go by bus/car
go by bike/motorbike
go by taxi/train
go on foot,
ride a bike/motorbike

TIME
45 minutes

Travel survey

Warmer

1 Put students in groups of three. Explain that you are going to have a competition to see who can name the most forms of transport (give *car* and *bus* as examples of transport) in two minutes.

2 Start the game, then stop the students after two minutes.

3 Check the answers, writing the different forms of transport on the board. The team with the most are the winners.

Input

1 Put students in pairs. Give each pair a copy of the word forks (Part A of the worksheet).

2 Ask them to complete the word forks with words from the Warmer. Explain that some words can go with more than one verb, and that they can add extra forks to the words if necessary.

3 Give out the remaining copies of the worksheet so that each student has a copy. Check answers, making sure that everyone has at least the collocations in bold below.

> **Answer key**
> **go by** bus/train/car/bike/taxi/coach/motorbike
> **go on** foot
> **catch a** bus/train/plane/ferry/boat
> **get/take a** bus/train/plane/taxi/coach
> **ride a** bike/motorbike
> **drive a** car/bus/tractor

Practice

1 Refer students to the travel survey (Part B). Ask the students to work in their pairs and decide which verb is appropriate for each question.

2 Give out the remaining copies of the worksheet so that each student has a copy. Check answers.

> **Answer key**
> **1** catch **2** going **3** ride **4** take **5** go **6** get / go **7** driven

3 Divide each pair into student A and student B. Ask all the student As to work together and all the student Bs to work together.

4 Within the two new groups, the students should mingle and ask each other the questions, making a note of everyone's answers on the survey sheet.

5 When the students have spoken to everyone in their group, ask them to return to their pairs. Ask each pair to pool their answers and compile a short written report. For example, they should write something like *two people caught a bus last week. Nine people usually go on holiday by plane.*

6 Conduct feedback by asking each pair to report one finding to the class.

Follow-up

1 Ask the students to think of other places they go (e.g. *the swimming pool, to visit relatives, the railway station*). Ask them to write two more questions of their own in the same style as the survey they have just done.

2 Then they should move around and ask each other their questions.

3 Conduct feedback.

🔵 See page 125–6 for the best games from the CD-ROM to play after this unit.

A Word forks

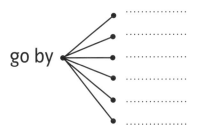

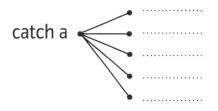

go on ——• ....

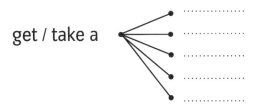

drive a ....

B Travel survey

Choose the correct work in italics in each question.

SURVEY!

1 When did you last *catch / go* a bus?

2 Do you like *going / catching* by plane?

3 Can you *ride / drive* a bike?

4 How often to you *go / take* a taxi?

5 Do you ever *run / go* to work or school on foot?

6 If you go to another city, do you prefer to *get / go* a train or *catch / go* by coach?

7 Have you ever *driven / ridden* a tractor?

9.2

Going for a drive

LEVEL
Intermediate

ACTIVITY TYPE
Bingo
Writing

MATERIALS
One Bingo grid (Part A of the worksheet) for each student for each round of Bingo One copy of the gap fill sentences (Part B) for each student

TARGET COLLOCATIONS
brake sharply,
car breaks down,
change gear,
dip your headlights,
give *someone* a lift,
heavy traffic,
increase speed,
look in the mirror,
lose your licence,
read the map,
sound the horn,
start the engine,
wear a seatbelt

TIME
45 minutes – 1 hour

Warmer

Put students in small groups (of 3–4). Explain that you have a list of things you do when driving and things that can happen when you drive. Ask them to work together to try and guess the things on the list. Elicit answers and write any that appear in the list of collocations on the board.

Input

1   Add any collocations that did not come up in the Warmer to the list on the board.

2   Give out a blank Bingo grid (Part A of the worksheet) to each student and explain that you are going to play a version of Bingo.

3   Ask students to choose four different collocations from the board and write one in each of the four squares on their grid. Explain that they should only choose collocations that they think they understand.

4   Start to read out the definitions (see below). When a student hears a definition for a collocation on their grid, they should cross it off.

5   The first person to cross off all four shouts 'Bingo!' and is the winner. Ask them to read out their collocations and check that they were correct.

6   Play the game as many times as appropriate.

7   Conduct feedback, making sure that everyone understands the meaning of all the collocations, then rub them off the board.

Bingo definitions

   1   This is what you get when there are too many cars on the roads.(*heavy traffic*)
   2   This is what might happen when there is something wrong with your car. (*car breaks down*)
   3   You might offer to do this if someone does not have a car. (*give someone a lift*)
   4   You have to do this when you are slowing down or speeding up. (*change gear*)
   5   You do this if you need to stop suddenly. (*brake sharply*)
   6   You should do this if someone is driving towards you at night.(*dip your headlights*)
   7   You might do this to warn someone of danger. (*sound the horn*)
   8   This could happen if the police catch you driving dangerously. (*lose your licence*)
   9   Passengers and drivers do this to make themselves safer when travelling. (*wear a seatbelt*)
   10 If you want to see what is behind you, you can do this. (*look in the mirror*)
   11 If you need to find the way, you can do this. (*read the map*)
   12 If you put your foot on the pedal and go faster, you do this. (*increase speed*)
   13 This happens when you turn the key to begin your journey. (*start the engine*)

Practice

1   Put the students in pairs and give each pair a copy of the gap fill sentences (Part B). Ask them to complete the sentences.

2   Give out the blank sentences to the other person in the pair so that each student has a copy. Check answers.

> **Answer key**
>
> **1** heavy   **2** lift   **3** seatbelt   **4** gear   **5** sharply   **6** headlight   **7** horn
> **8** licence   **9** start   **10** look   **11** read   **12** car   **13** speed

Follow-up

1   Put students in groups of three to four. Ask them to write a short story involving a car journey. Each person in the group should write an opening sentence. Then they pass the paper to the person on their right, and they all write a second sentence.

2   Allow each person to write at least two sentences on each paper. Give a warning when you are going to end the exercise so that the students can write a concluding sentence.

3   Allow students time to read and discuss the stories they wrote.

🔵 See page 125–6 for the best games from the CD-ROM to play after this unit.

A Bingo grids

(blank grid)

✂ -

(blank grid)

✂ -

B Complete the gap fill sentences.

1 I was late home from work because of .... traffic.

2 She offered to give me a .... to the station.

3 In the UK, all drivers and passengers have to wear a ....

4 I changed .... as we approached the turning.

5 I had to brake .... when a dog ran into the road.

6 The driver of the car coming towards me forgot to dip his ....

7 I sounded the .... to warn him about the danger.

8 If you are caught driving dangerously, you can lose your ....

9 When it is very cold, it can be hard to .... the engine.

10 Before you turn, you should always .... in the mirror.

11 I asked Adam if he would .... the map for me.

12 My .... broke down on the way to London.

13 You can increase your .... when there isn't much traffic on the road.

9.3

Further afield

LEVEL
Advanced

ACTIVITY TYPE
Reading
Writing clues
Board game

MATERIALS
One copy of the
frequently asked
questions and
answers (Part A of
the worksheet), cut
up as cards and
shuffled, for each
pair
One copy of the
abbreviations grid
(Part B) for each
student
One copy of the
appropriate list of
collocations (Part C)
for each team
member

**TARGET
COLLOCATIONS**
board a plane,
break your journey,
connecting flight,
go through security,
internal flight,
issue *someone* with
a boarding card,
long-haul flight,
pass through passport
control,
point of departure,
reclaim your baggage,
short-haul flight,
travel light

TIME
45 minutes – 1 hour

Warmer

Lead a five-minute whole-class discussion about flying and airports. Ask students if they like flying. Ask if anyone has ever had a problem flying, e.g. *missing a flight*, or *losing their baggage*.

Input

1 Put students in pairs and give each pair a set of cards with the frequently asked questions and answers (Part A of the worksheet).

2 Ask students to match the questions to the answers.

3 Check answers. Ask students to focus on the collocations in bold. Make sure they understand them.

Practice

1 Divide the class into three teams, called teams 1, 2 and 3. Give each team the abbreviations grid and their team's collocations (Parts B and C of the worksheet).

2 Ask each team to work together to write a set of clues for their collocations. Give an example of a simple, related collocation, to show them how to do it, e.g. **MF** is when you arrive too late and the plane has already gone (answer: *miss your flight*). Make sure that all the students in each team write the clues down, and that all the students know that articles and possessive pronouns are missing from the abbreviations.

3 When all three teams have finished, create new groups of three consisting of one student each from teams 1, 2 and 3. Each student should have a pen of a different colour.

4 The three students take turns to read a clue from their group of words, and the other two students race to answer. The student who gets that answer first 'wins' the square, and circles it in their colour. The student with the most squares at the end is the winner.

Follow-up

In pairs, have students tell each other about the best and the worst journey they have ever had. They should choose one of their experiences and write a paragraph about it.

● See page 125–6 for the best games from the CD-ROM to play after this unit.

A Frequently asked questions for passengers taking connecting flights

I am transferring from one international flight to another at London Heathrow. Will I need a UK visa?	If you are connecting from one international flight to another, you do not need a UK visa. Your passport will be checked but you will not need to **pass through passport control**.
*Will I have enough time to catch my **connecting flight**?*	Yes, your airline will have calculated that you have enough time. You will need to **go through security** and make sure you arrive at the gate in time or you may not be allowed to **board the plane.**
Where do I get my boarding card for the connecting flight?	You should be **issued with** all **boarding cards** at your original **point of departure**. If you do not have a boarding card go to your airline's desk.
*Can I **break my journey in London?***	You will need to check with your travel company to see if your ticket allows this. You will also need to make sure that your passport or visa allows entry to the UK.
How long should I allow to get out of the airport at my final destination?	This will vary according to how busy the airport is. However, if you are short of time, we recommend that you **travel light** – if you do not need to **reclaim baggage**, you will be able to leave more quickly.
How long before my first flight should I arrive at the airport?	As a rule, allow two hours for **short-haul flights**, three hours for **long-haul flights** and ninety minutes for **internal flights**. However, you should always check with your travel company.

B

IF	L-H F	TL	RB
PTPC	BP	S-H F	IWBC
CF	GTS	POD	BJ

C Collocations

TEAM 1	TEAM 2	TEAM 3
• internal flight • board a plane • reclaim your baggage • point of departure	• pass through passport control • issue someone with a boarding card • short-haul flight • break your journey	• connecting flight • go through security • long-haul flight • travel light

Doctor, doctor

LEVEL
Elementary /
Pre-intermediate

ACTIVITY TYPE
Board game

MATERIALS
One copy of the
worksheet board
game, for each pair
of students
A coin and three
coloured counters
for each group of
three

**TARGET
COLLOCATIONS**
break your arm,
break your leg,
call an ambulance,
feel sick,
have (got) a cold,
have an operation,
go into hospital,
leave hospital,
take a tablet,
take medicine

TIME
40–50 minutes

Warmer

Explain that you are going to be talking about health, and what happens when you become ill or have an injury. Elicit some of the vocabulary for this unit by asking the class to suggest some types of illness and injury, and asking them where they go for treatment.

Input

1   Put students in pairs, and give each pair a copy of the board game.

2   Ask students to work together to describe what is happening in the pictures, using the verbs. Tell students that some verbs are used more than once.

3   Check answers, and write the correct collocations up on the board.

Practice

1   Put students in groups of three.

2   Give each group a coin, and give each person a different coloured counter.

3   Tell students they are going to play the board game and explain the rules/demonstrate the game:

  ● Students take it in turns to toss or spin the coin. If the coin lands on 'heads', they move forward one square, and if it lands on 'tails' they move forward two squares.

  ● If a student lands on a picture square, they should say what is happening in the picture.

  ● If they land on a square with a verb in it, they must make a sentence connected with health and hospitals using that verb. Tell the students that they must not repeat a sentence their opponents have used (they can use the same collocation, but must vary the sentence in some way).

  ● The other students in the group judge whether the descriptions and sentences are correct.

  ● If they are correct, the student moves forward an extra square. If they are incorrect, the student stays where they are until the next go.

  ● The winner is the person who finishes first.

Follow-up

1   Ask each student to write a short story using at least four of the collocations they have learned, but leaving gaps where the collocations should go. Encourage them to be as creative as possible, e.g. explaining what someone ate that made them *feel sick,* or what they were doing when they *broke their leg.*

2   When they have finished, ask students to swap stories and fill in the missing collocations.

● See page 125–6 for the best games from the CD-ROM to play after this unit.

In good health

LEVEL
Intermediate

ACTIVITY TYPE
Jigsaw reading
Role play

MATERIALS
One copy of the pictures (Part A of the worksheet)
One copy of Text A and Text B (Part B) and the list of comprehension questions (Part C) for each student

TARGET COLLOCATIONS
check *someone's* blood pressure,
dull ache,
fall ill,
feel *someone's* pulse,
heavy cold,
make an appointment,
runny nose,
sharp pain,
sore throat,
splitting headache,
take *someone's* temperature,
write a prescription

TIME
40–50 minutes

Warmer

Explain that you are going to be talking about health and going to the doctor's. Ask the class to brainstorm some words and phrases connected with illnesses and injuries, and the things doctors and nurses do.

Input

1   Put the class into two teams.

2   Ask one student from each team to come to the front of the class. Show the two students one of the pictures and ask them to mime the picture shown on the card to the rest of their team to guess. Award a point to the first team to guess the collocation.

3   If neither team can guess the exact collocation, ask questions to try and elicit it. For example, ask, *What is another way of saying 'to become ill'?* for *fall ill*, or *What do we call a heavy sort of pain that lasts for a long time?* for *dull ache*.

4   When a collocation has been guessed or elicited, write it on the board.

5   Continue the game with the next card and two more students (one from each team).

Practice

1   Put the students in pairs. Give one student in each pair Text 1 and the other student Text 2. Also give each pair a list of comprehension questions (Part C of the worksheet). Ask each student to read their text and answer the comprehension questions on it without looking at the other person's text. The texts are similar but there are several differences.

2   Now explain to the pairs that they have both read texts which are similar but have eight differences. Ask them to discuss their answers to the comprehension questions and try to find out the differences.

3   Give out the remaining Tom texts and comprehensions questions so that each student has a copy. Check answers.

Answer key

1   Tom (1) was on holiday but Tom (2) was at work when he fell ill.

2   Tom (1)'s foot felt better in the night, while Tom (2) was kept awake by the pain in his foot.

3   Tom (1) woke up with a sore throat and a runny nose, while Tom (2) had earache and a splitting headache.

4   Tom (1)'s doctor took his temperature and checked his blood pressure, while Tom (2)'s doctor took his temperature and felt his pulse.

5   Tom (1) had a heavy cold but Tom (2) had an infection.

6   Tom (1) had no medicine but Tom (2) was given antibiotics.

7   Tom (1) had a drawing pin in his shoe, while Tom (2) had a nail in his.

8   Tom (1)'s doctor was a woman, Tom (2)'s was a man. (This is a bit of a trick point – they know this only from the pronoun used.)

Follow-up

1   Ask students to work in pairs to write the outline of a role play in a doctor's surgery. The outline should not state the doctor's and patient's actual words, but suggest what they might say. For example, *Doctor: asks the patient to sit down*.

2   When the pairs have finished, they should swap their outline with another pair. Each pair should now act out the role plays.

● See page 125–6 for the best games from the CD-ROM to play after this unit.

A

 feel someone's pulse	 take someone's temperature	 sore throat	 fall ill
 check someone's blood pressure	 sharp pain	 heavy cold	 write a prescription
 runny nose	 make an appointment	 splitting headache	 dull ache

B

Text 1

Tom was on holiday when he **fell ill**. First, he felt a **sharp pain** in his foot. The pain got worse and worse. In the night, his foot was a bit better, but he woke up the next day with a **sore throat** and a **runny nose**. During the morning, the pain in his foot got worse again, so he decided to **make an appointment** to see the doctor. The doctor examined his foot and his arm, **took his temperature** and checked **his blood pressure**. 'There's nothing much wrong,' she said. 'You simply have a **heavy cold**. Go home and rest.' 'But what about the pain in my foot?' said Tom. 'Surely that can't be to do with my cold.' 'No, it isn't,' the doctor replied. 'You have a drawing pin stuck in the bottom of your shoe.'

Text 2

Tom was at work when he **fell ill**. First, he felt a **sharp pain** in his foot. The pain got worse and worse. In the night, his foot kept him awake with a **dull ache**, and he got up the next day with an earache and a **splitting headache**. During the morning, the pain in his foot got worse and worse, so he decided to **make an appointment** to see the doctor. The doctor examined his foot and his arm, **took his temperature** and **felt his pulse**. 'You have a nasty ear infection,' he said. 'I'll **write you a prescription** for some antibiotics.' 'But what about the pain in my foot?' said Tom. 'Surely that can't be to do with my ear infection.' 'No, it isn't,' the doctor replied. 'You have a nail stuck in the bottom of your shoe.'

C Answer the questions about the text you read.

1 Where was Tom when he fell ill?
2 What symptoms did he have?
3 How did he feel the next morning?
4 What did the doctor do?

5 What did the doctor say was wrong with Tom?
6 Did the doctor write Tom a prescription?
7 What did the doctor say about Tom's foot?
8 Was the doctor a man or a woman?

10.3

A healthy mind

LEVEL
Advanced

ACTIVITY TYPE
Crossword

MATERIALS
One copy of the
multiple-choice
questions (Part A
of the worksheet)
for each pair
One copy of the
crossword grid and
either the Across
collocations *or* the
Down collocations
(Part B) for each pair

**TARGET
COLLOCATIONS**
admit someone to
hospital,
adverse reaction,
dress a wound,
experience side effects,
heavily sedated,
in a critical condition,
in a stable condition,
infectious disease,
sprain your ankle,
symptoms persist,
take an overdose,
undergo treatment

TIME
45 minutes – 1 hour

Warmer

Go through the alphabet. For each letter of the alphabet, ask students to call out a word connected with illness, injury, hospitals or doctors (e.g., *anaesthetic, backache, cold, doctor, emergency*).

Input

1 Put students in pairs. Give each pair a copy of the multiple-choice sentences (Part A of the worksheet). Ask students to work together to choose the correct option.

2 Give out the remaining copies of the multiple-choice statements so that each student has a copy. Check answers.

> **Answer key**
>
> | | | | |
> |---|---|---|---|
> | **1** | symptoms persist | **7** | an infectious disease |
> | **2** | undergoing treatment | **8** | heavily sedated |
> | **3** | critical condition | **9** | an adverse reaction |
> | **4** | stable condition | **10** | dress a wound |
> | **5** | admitted to hospital | **11** | taken an overdose |
> | **6** | experiencing side effects | **12** | sprain your ankle |

Practice

1 Put students in new pairs. Give half the pairs a copy of a crossword grid and the Across collocations and the other half a crossword and the Down collocations.

2 First, ask each pair to fill in the words in bold on their crossword.

3 Then, ask them to write, on a separate sheet of paper, a sentence for each of their collocations, but leaving a space where the word in bold (which is now in the crossword) would go. For example, for 10 across, they might write something like *If you trip over a step, you could .... your ankle.*

4 When they have finished, ask each pair to swap their crossword and gap fill sentences with a pair who had the other set of collocations. They then fill in the gaps in the sentences, and use them to complete the crossword.

Follow-up

1 Ask one student to stand with their back to the board. The teacher writes one of the collocations from the unit on the board.

2 The rest of the class try to explain the collocation, until the person standing guesses which one it is.

3 Continue the game with the other collocations, asking a different student to come to the front for each collocation.

⊘ See page 125–6 for the best games from the CD-ROM to play after this unit.

A Choose the correct collocation in these sentences.

1. If you continue to feel ill, we say your **symptoms endure / symptoms persist / symptoms repeat.**

2. If you are visiting a doctor and taking medicine for an illness, we say you are **taking treatment / tolerating treatment / undergoing treatment.**

3. If someone is so ill that it is possible they might die, we say they are in a **terrible condition / lifeless condition / critical condition.**

4. If a very ill person has been treated so that they are not getting worse and are not likely to die, we say they are in a **stable condition / fair condition / pleasant condition.**

5. If a doctor has decided that you need to stay in hospital, we say you are **allowed to hospital / admitted to hospital / accepted to hospital.**

6. If a medicine you are taking has unwanted and unexpected results, we say you are **experiencing disadvantages / experiencing side actions / experiencing side effects.**

7. If someone has a disease that can spread to others, we say it is **an infectious disease / a contaminating disease / a spreading disease.**

8. If someone is given drugs to make them very sleepy, we say they are **greatly sedated / heavily sedated / heavily under sedation.**

9. If you become more ill after being given a drug, we say you have had **a bad reaction / a negative reaction / an adverse reaction.**

10. If you put a bandage on a wound, we say you **dress a wound / pad a wound / wind a wound.**

11. If someone takes too much of a drug, we say they have **taken an overdose / eaten an overdose / swallowed an overdose.**

12. If you twist your ankle and hurt it badly, we say you have **wrenched your ankle / sprained your ankle / torn your ankle.**

B Crossword

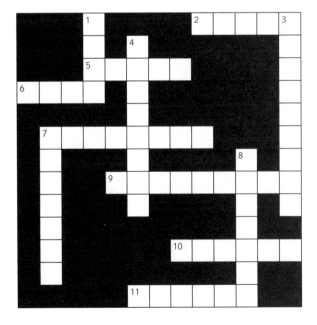

Across collocations:

2. **admit** someone to hospital
5. **dress** a wound
6. **take** an overdose
7. **symptoms** persist
9. in a critical **condition**
10. **sprain** your ankle
11. in a **stable** condition

Down collocations:

1. experience **side** effects
3. undergo **treatment**
4. an adverse **reaction**
7. heavily **sedated**
8. an infectious **disease**

11.1

The world of work

LEVEL
Elementary /
Pre-intermediate

ACTIVITY TYPE
Board game

MATERIALS
One copy of the
worksheet board
game and game
cards (cut up) for
each group of three
students
One dice for each
group and some
way of measuring
thirty seconds (a
clock on the wall
with a minute hand
is ideal, but
otherwise provide
clocks/egg timers or
ask the students to
use their own
watches)
Coins and counters

**TARGET
COLLOCATIONS**
a high salary,
a low salary,
be badly paid,
be well paid,
earn money,
get a new job,
have an interview,
look for a job,
lose your job,
work hard

TIME
40–50 minutes

Warmer

Tell the class that they will be learning about words to do with work. Elicit the questions *What is your job?* and *What do you do?* by writing *I'm a teacher* on the board. Then elicit the question *Where do you work?* by writing *I work in a (language) school.* Highlight the noun *job* and the verb *work*.

Input

1 Write the collocations on the board and next to them draw three columns. Put a tick at the top of the first column, a cross at the top of the second, and a dash at the top of the third.

2 Put the students in pairs. Ask the students to copy the columns. Then ask them to put the collocations that refer to good things in the first column, those that refer to bad things in the second column, and those which refer to neither bad nor good things in the third. (You may like to teach the word *neutral*.) Explain that there may be some disagreement – *hard work* for example might be a good thing for some people and a bad thing for others.

3 Conduct feedback.

Practice

1 Put the students in groups of three. Give each group a copy of the board, a set of cards (you may want to enlarge the board on the photocopier) and a coin, and give each student a coloured counter.

2 Tell the students that they are going to play the board game and explain the rules/ demonstrate the game:

   ● Students take it in turns to toss or spin the coin. If the coin lands on *heads*, they move forward one square, and if it lands on *tails* they move forward two squares.

   ● If a player lands on an instruction square, they should move the required number of squares.

   ● If they land on a blank square, they have to pick up a card and answer the question on it. If they answer the question satisfactorily, they move one space forward. If they answer incorrectly or cannot answer the question, they move back a space. The other players in the group judge whether they have answered correctly.

   ● Once a player has followed the instruction on one instruction square, or picked up one card and answered the question, play moves to the next player.

   ● The first player to reach the end is the winner.

Follow-up

1 Ask the students to sit in a circle. Everyone has to think of one fact that relates to a member of their family's job or a friend's job, and that includes one of the collocations they have used in the lesson.

2 The youngest student in the group whispers their fact to the person on their left (e.g. '*My father got a new job last year*'). The person on the left reports the fact in a whisper to the person on their left, (e.g. *Pilar's father got a new job last year*). This carries on until the whisper reaches the student on Pilar's right, who reports what she or he thought she heard.

3 Repeat this activity with different members of the group.

● See page 125–6 for the best games from the CD-ROM to play after this unit.

Board game

START 1	2	You get a new job! (Go forward five spaces.) 3	4	You are badly paid. (Go back two spaces.) 5
6	You have a low salary. (Go back two spaces.) 7	8	You earn a lot of money. (Go forward two spaces.) 9	10
You work too hard. (Go back four spaces) 11	12	You start looking for a job. (Go forward one space.) 13	14	You lose your job. (Go back seven spaces) 15
16	You have an interview! (Go forward two spaces.) 17	18	You are badly paid. (Go back five spaces) 19	20
You are well paid. (Go forward two spaces.) 21	22	You lose your job. (Go back three spaces) 23	24	You have a high salary! (Go forward two spaces.) 25
26	You get a new job. (Go back two spaces.) 27	28	You are badly paid. (Go back two spaces.) 29	FINISH 30

Game cards

Name 3 jobs.	Say 3 things you do in an office.	He / She produces food to sell.	Name a job beginning with 'd'.	Someone who works with animals
Name two pieces of office equipment.	Someone who works in a hospital	He / She looks after your health	Say 2 good things about work.	Say 2 bad things about work.
Name a job beginning with 't'.	Name a job beginning with 'n'.	Name a job beginning with 's'.	Someone who works with children	Say 3 things you do in an office.
Say a word meaning 'the money that you earn by working'.	Someone whose job is keeping people safe	Someone who works with food	Someone whose job involves driving	Name four jobs.

11.2

LEVEL
Intermediate

ACTIVITY TYPE
Jigsaw reading
Writing definitions

MATERIALS
One copy of the
picture (Part A of the
worksheet) for each
pair
One copy of Dan's
story and Dan's
boss's story (Parts B
and C)
One copy of the
comprehension
questions (Part D)
for each student
One copy of the
collocations (Part E)
for each pair

**TARGET
COLLOCATIONS**
apply for a job,
demanding work,
give up a job,
heavy workload,
highly qualified,
join a company,
leave a company,
long hours,
member of staff,
reach a target,
set up a business,
suffer from stress

TIME
30–45 minutes

Overworked?

Warmer

1   Tell the class that you are going to be talking about work today.

2   Put students in pairs and give each pair a copy of the picture and allow them five minutes to discuss what they think is happening in the picture. Elicit that the man is unhappy/anxious/stressed and discuss the reasons he might be unhappy.

Input

1   Have students work individually. Give half the class a copy of Dan's story and the other half a copy of Dan's boss's story. Give everyone a copy of the comprehension questions.

2   Allow each student ten minutes to read the text and answer the questions. Students can use a dictionary if necessary.

3   When they have finished, ask students to check their answers with another student who read the same text.

Answer key

	Dan's story	Dan's boss's story
1	3 years ago	3 years ago
2	He was exhausted and suffering from stress	He doesn't know why he left the company
3	Yes, he always reached his targets	Yes, he was a valuable member of staff and highly qualified
4	No, he never thanked him	Yes, see comments above
5	Not difficult but a very heavy workload and long hours	Sales is demanding work
6	50 hours minimum	Not more than 40 hours
7	Applied for lots of jobs	Set up his own business

4   Put students in pairs with a partner who read a different text from them. Ask the students to compare their answers and then to write down four points where Dan's story and Dan's boss's story do not agree with each other.

Answer key

1   Dan did not feel that his boss valued him, but his boss said he did value him.

2   Dan said the work wasn't difficult, but that there was a heavy workload and the hours were long. Dan's boss said the work was demanding.

3   Dan said he worked a minimum of 50 hours a week, but Dan's boss said no one worked more than 40.

4   Dan said he's applied for a lot of jobs but is still unemployed. Dan's boss thought he had set up his own business.

Practice

1   Keep the students in their new pairs. Make half the pairs group A, and the other half group B. Give each pair a copy of the collocations (Part E of the worksheet).

2   Ask group A pairs to write definitions for the collocations in box A, and group B pairs to write definitions for the collocations in box B. (Both halves of each pair must write down the definitions.)

3   Now put the class in new pairs, so that each group A student is with a group B student. Ask each pair to take it in turns reading out their definitions for their partner to guess.

Follow-up

In their pairs, students use the collocations to talk about work experience they have had.

⊙ See page 125–6 for the best games from the CD-ROM to play after this unit.

A

✂--

B

Dan's story

I **gave up** my **job** after three years' working for the company because I was exhausted and **suffering from stress**. I worked really hard and always **reached** my **targets** week after week but I never got any thanks for it.

Working in sales wasn't difficult but I had such a **heavy workload**. I mean, I've worked **long hours** in my previous jobs but this was ridiculous – 50 hours a week minimum, just to get the work done.

In the end I decided to leave for the sake of my health. I've **applied for** a lot of **jobs** but haven't even had one interview. Now, six months later, I'm still unemployed.

✂

C

Dan's boss's story

Dan **joined the company** three years ago. I have no idea why he **left** the **company**. We were very disappointed to lose him as he was a very valuable **member of staff** and **highly qualified**.

Sales is very **demanding work** but Dan always seemed so happy here. And the conditions are good too – I know for a fact that none of our staff works more than 40 hours a week.

I haven't seen Dan since he resigned six months ago. Someone told me that he had **set up** his own **business**. Good luck to him.

✂--

D Answer the questions about the text you read.

1 When did Dan join the company?
2 Why did he give up his job?
3 Was Dan good at his job?
4 Did Dan's boss value him?
5 What was the job like?
6 How many hours a week did he work?
7 What has Dan done since he left the company?

✂--

E Collocations

A	B
give up a job: reach a target: long hours: join a company: member of staff: demanding work:	suffer from stress: leave a company: heavy workload: highly qualified: apply for a job: set up a business:

11.3

Work stories

LEVEL
Advanced

ACTIVITY TYPE
Matching collocations
and definitions
Storywriting
Mingle

MATERIALS
One copy of the
sentences and
definitions (Part A of
the worksheet) for
each student
One individual
picture (from Part B)
for each group

**TARGET
COLLOCATIONS**
a high turnover of
staff,
hand in your notice,
highly motivated,
high-powered job,
land a job,
lay off staff,
manual labour,
menial task,
on-the-job training,
seek promotion,
take on staff,
unpaid overtime,
unsocial hours

TIME
45 minutes

Warmer

1 Depending on your students' experience, ask them to think for a few minutes about their first jobs or their dream jobs. Then have them talk to a partner about their dream or first job.

2 Ask some students to report back on what their partner said.

Input

1 Put students in pairs. Give each pair Part A of the worksheet. Point out the collocations in bold and ask them to match up the definitions below the sentences with the collocations.

2 Give out the remaining copies of Part A so that each student has a copy. Conduct whole-class feed back and check understanding.

> **Answer key**
> **1** g **2** e **3** b **4** d **5** c **6** k **7** f **8** m **9** h **10** i **11** a **12** j **13** l

Practice

1 Put students in groups of four. Give each group one picture (from Part B) and ask them to keep it secret.

2 Ask each group to choose five of the collocations from Part A and to construct a work story that somehow incorporates the picture they have been given. The idea is to incorporate the item shown in the picture in such a way that no one can easily guess what it is. (It may help to introduce the idea of a *red herring* – meaning another possible word that students might guess is the mystery word.)

3 Now regroup the students so that each group has one member from each of the previous groups.

4 Within each group, have students take it in turns to read out their story. The other group members try to guess what the picture was.

Follow-up

1 Ask each student to choose a collocation from the lesson and write it on a piece of paper. Ask them to think of a sentence which contains a paraphrase or definition of the collocation from which another student could guess the collocation. For example, for *hand in your notice* they might say, *I'm going to tell my boss I don't want to work here any more.*

2 Then ask the students to stand up and mingle. When they meet another student, they should say their sentence. The other student guesses the collocation and the pair then reverse roles.

3 When both students have had a go, the pair exchange collocations and each find a different student to speak to.

● See page 125–6 for the best games from the CD-ROM to play after this unit.

A Match the collocations in bold in sentences 1–13 with the definitions given below (a–m).

1 In these bad economic conditions, many firms are having to **lay off staff**.
2 Call centres have a very **high turnover of staff**.
3 On the one hand, teachers have long holidays. On the other hand, they do a lot of **unpaid overtime**.
4 When doctors are training they **work** very **unsocial hours**.
5 Both companies are expanding and have **taken on** a lot of new **staff**.
6 He's just **landed a job** with a big City bank.
7 Most posts involve an element of **on-the-job training**.
8 If the job doesn't improve I'm going to **hand in my notice**.
9 He gets offended if I ask him to do **menial tasks** such as typing up letters.
10 The advert says 'highly motivated, energetic staff required'.
11 Being a gardener involves a lot of **manual labour**.
12 I've only been in this job a year so I'm not **seeking promotion** yet.
13 His wife has a very **high-powered job** as a lawyer.

a work that involves your hands
b extra hours that you work for which you are not paid
c to employ new people
d to work very late at night or very early in the morning
e when a company's staff change very frequently
f training while a person is working
g to stop employing people because there is not enough work for them
h boring work that does not require much skill
i extremely keen to work hard
j to try to get a more important or better-paid job in the same company
k to succeed in getting a good job
l a very important and demanding job probably with stress
m to tell an employer that you are going to leave your job

B

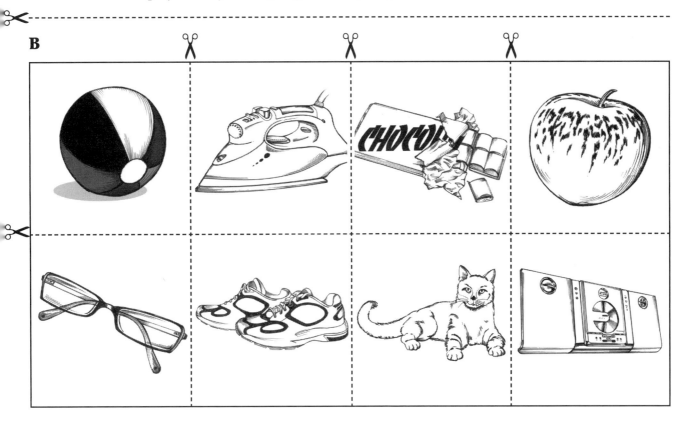

12.1

LEVEL
Elementary /
Pre-intermediate

ACTIVITY TYPE
Discussion
Gap fill

MATERIALS
One copy of the
sentence halves
(Part A of the
worksheet) cut up
into slips for each
pair
One copy of the
completed
sentences (Part A)
for each student
One copy of the gap
fill (Part B) for each
pair

**TARGET
COLLOCATIONS**
borrow money,
earn money,
get paid,
lend money,
make money,
pay a bill,
pay by credit card,
pay tax,
pay the rent,
save money,
spend money,
take credit cards

TIME
35–45 minutes

Money money money!

Warmer

1   Put students in pairs. In their pairs, ask them to discuss what they like spending money on.

2   Ask some of the students to report back to the class.

Input

1   Keep the students in their pairs. Give each pair a copy of the sentence halves. Ask them to make twelve sentences by matching the sentence halves.

2   Check answers and then give each student a copy of the completed sentences.

3   Now ask the pairs to discuss whether they think the statements are true or not.

4   Ask different pairs what they decided about each statement and discuss as a class.

Practice

1   Give each student a copy of the gap fill and ask them to fill the gaps of the paragraph with the verbs in the correct form.

2   Ask the students to check their answers with a partner.

3   Check answers.

> **Answer key**
> 1 save   2 earn   3 paid   4 paid   5 spending   6 pay   7 pay   8 take
> 9 lend   10 makes   11 borrow

Follow-up

1   Put the students in pairs and ask them to prepare their own gap fill exercise with different sentences for the collocations they have learned.

2   Ask each pair to swap their exercise with another pair and then complete the other pair's exercise.

   See page 125–6 for the best games from the CD-ROM to play after this unit.

A Sentence halves

Footballers	**earn** too much **money**.
You can **make** a lot of **money**	working in a bank.
Teachers **get paid**	a lot of money.
I **spend** a lot of **money**	on clothes.
It's a good idea to	**save money**.
I never **lend money**	to my friends.
I never **borrow money**	from my friends.
I **pay**	too much **tax**.
I always **pay** my **bills**	as soon as they arrive.
I don't have enough money to	**pay the rent**.
I usually **pay** for things	**by credit card**.
Most shops	**take credit cards**.

B Complete the paragraph below with these verbs in the correct form.

pay	take	earn	pay	make	spend	pay	save	borrow	lend	pay

I'd like to buy my own house one day so I'm trying to (1) .... a little money each month. It's difficult because I don't (2) .... very much money. After I've (3) .... tax and (4) .... the rent I don't have much left.

I also really like (5) .... money, especially on clothes and holidays. I usually (6) .... by credit card, but I always (7) .... the monthly bill immediately. I don't like to carry money with me, so I'm glad that most shops (8) .... credit cards these days.

My dad said he will (9) .... me some money. He has a very successful business and it (10) .... a lot of money. But I don't really like to (11) .... money from him. It's very nice of him but I'd prefer to be independent.

12.2

LEVEL
Intermediate

ACTIVITY TYPE
Finding collocations
in texts
Giving advice
Role play

MATERIALS
One copy of the
worksheet for each
student

**TARGET
COLLOCATIONS**
annual salary,
bring in money,
careful with money,
get a loan,
have an overdraft,
highly paid,
leave a tip,
make a living,
owe money,
pay interest,
pay off a loan,
pay well,
poorly paid,
steady income

TIME
45 minutes

Short of money

Warmer

1 Put students in pairs. Ask them to discuss what they think are the most common problems that people usually have with money. Are people's problems different at different stages in their life?

2 Ask several students to report back to the class about what they discussed.

Input

1 Explain to students that they are going to read four paragraphs describing four people's financial problems. Give a copy of the worksheet to each student.

2 Ask students to read the four texts and answer the comprehension questions about them. Explain that they should use information from the text to explain their answers.

3 Ask students to check their answers in pairs.

4 Check answers as a whole class, make sure that the answers include the collocations (see answer key) and write the collocations on the board.

Answer key

1 She had a good **annual salary**.
2 She **has an overdraft**.
3 You have to **pay interest** on them.
4 His job is **poorly paid**.
5 They **leave a tip**.
6 He is **careful with money**.
7 Lena **got a loan**.
8 She doesn't like **owing money**.
9 It will be **highly paid**.
10 She will **pay off** her **loan**.
11 She doesn't have a **steady income**.
12 The acting work **pays well** but she doesn't get enough of it.
13 No. She says it **brings in** a little **money**.
14 No. She finds it hard to **make a living**.

5 Give them five minutes in their pairs to decide who they feel most sorry for. Have a class vote to see who is considered to be in the worst situation and discuss the reasons.

Practice

1 Put students in pairs. Make half the pairs group A and the other half group B.

2 Explain that the students are now going to think of some advice that they can give to Saskia, Erik, Lena and Alicia about how to improve their financial situation. Ask group A pairs to focus on Saskia and Erik and ask group B to focus on Lena and Alicia.

3 Ask pairs to discuss their ideas, and make a note of their ideas. (All students should make notes.)

4 Now put the students into new pairs so that a student from group A is working with a student from group B.

5 Ask the students to do a role play, with student A playing the financial advisor (referring to their notes) and student B playing Saskia.

6 Ask the students to do a second role play, this time with student B playing the financial advisor and student A playing Lena.

Follow-up

1 If students enjoyed the role plays, put them with a new partner and ask them to do the two remaining role plays.

2 Alternatively, ask students to write a paragraph, explaining the advice they gave in the Practice above.

● See page 125–6 for the best games from the CD-ROM to play after this unit.

Saskia

I've just lost my job and have now got serious money problems. I used to work in a bank where I had a good annual salary. Then suddenly I lost my job, but still had all the same bills to pay.

The only way I can pay my bills now is by having a huge overdraft. And the thing about overdrafts is that you have to pay interest on them, so my financial situation is getting worse all the time.

1 What does Saskia say about her salary in her old job in the bank?
2 How does she pay her bills now?
3 What does she say is the problem with overdrafts?

Erik

I work as a waiter in a small restaurant although it is very poorly paid. Some weeks are better than others, but it really depends on tips. It really helps when my customers leave a tip. But, unfortunately, not everyone leaves a tip.

It can be a struggle, bringing up a family on such a low wage, but I manage. I'm very careful with money so we survive.

4 What does Erik say about his job?
5 How do some of his customers help him?
6 How does Erik manage?

Lena

I worry about money all the time. I'm studying to be a doctor. It's a long, expensive training and I don't have rich parents so I have to pay for it myself. I've had to get a huge loan, which I'm not very happy about as I don't like owing money. In three years' time though I should have a highly paid job and I'll be able to pay off my loan within a couple of years. Until then I'll just have to study hard and live simply.

7 How does Lena pay for her studies?
6 Why is she not happy about this?
9 How does she describe her future job?
10 What will she do when she starts earning money?

Alicia

I'm an actress and my problem is that I don't have a steady income. When I get some acting work, it pays well, but often I don't work for five or six months at a time and obviously I'm not earning during that time. I do a little teaching work in between acting jobs, which brings in a little money, but it's not much and I find it hard to make a living.

11 What does Alicia feel is her main problem with money?
12 What does she say about the pay for acting work?
13 Does her teaching work earn her much money?
14 Does she earn enough money to live?

Good with money?

LEVEL
Advanced

ACTIVITY TYPE
Gap fill
Reading
Role play

MATERIALS
One copy of the gap
fill + collocations
(Part A of the
worksheet) for each
student
One copy of both
texts (Part B) for
each pair

**TARGET
COLLOCATIONS**
bargain hunting,
big-ticket item,
cost a fortune,
dirt cheap,
expensive tastes,
false economy,
hard-earned cash,
part with your cash,
pay over the odds,
spend a fortune,
value for money

TIME
45 minutes

Warmer

Ask *Are you a spender or a saver?* Discuss the answers together as a class.

Input

1   Put students in pairs. Give each pair the gap fill sentences (Part A of the worksheet). Ask them to complete the sentences, using the collocations in the correct form.

2   Give out the remaining copies of the worksheet so that each student has a copy and check answers.

> **Answer key**
>
> **1** dirt cheap   **2** part with their cash   **3** spent a fortune   **4** a false economy
> **5** big ticket items   **6** value for money   **7** hard-earned cash   **8** paid over the odds
> **9** expensive tastes   **10** cost a fortune   **11** bargain hunting

Practice

1   Give each student a copy of *A couple's attitude to money* (Part B of the worksheet). Explain that a husband and wife have been interviewed separately about their attitudes to money.

2   Have students read through the texts and answer the questions.

3   Ask students to compare their answers with a partner.

4   Check answers.

> **Answer key**
>
> **1**   He likes **bargain hunting** and getting value for money. She considers quality more than the price.
>
> **2**   No, according to her, he doesn't like **parting with his cash**, and according to him, he wants to keep hold of his **hard-earned cash**.
>
> **3**   Sue wanted to buy one with a famous name (which according to Ben **cost a fortune**). He said this was **paying over the odds** so they bought a **dirt cheap** one instead.
>
> **4**   It was a **false economy** because they had to **spend a fortune** getting it repaired.

Follow-up

Put the students in pairs. Ask one to assume the character of Ben and one to be Sue. Ask them to read through the texts once more, to turn the texts over and to discuss what they have said about each other. Encourage them to elaborate on what was said in the texts, making up more details about their behaviour in relation to money.

See page 125–6 for the best games from the CD-ROM to play after this unit.

A Complete the sentences with the correct form of a collocation from the box.

> bargain hunting , big-ticket item, cost a fortune, dirt cheap, expensive tastes, false economy, hard-earned cash,
> part with your cash, pay over the odds, spend a fortune, value for money

1 Travelling is a lot cheaper these days and you can pick up some .... flights if you shop around.
2 Sales staff have to try very hard to persuade people to .... their ....
3 They .... a .... on their wedding – the clothes, the food, the drink, everything was perfect.
4 It's a .... buying cheap clothes as they fall apart when you start wearing them.
5 We have some money set aside for the .... like cars, televisions and holidays.
6 This is good food and at £10 a head it represents great ....
7 You should check the quality of the goods before handing over your ....
8 I think I .... the .... for my new computer. If I'd shopped around, I'm sure I'd have got it cheaper somewhere else.
9 Her clothes are all designer labels so she has very ....
10 His car must have .... a .... ! How do you think he can afford it?
11 I love .... in the January sales.

✂--

B A couple's attitude to money

Read the two texts below and then answer the following questions. Where possible, for each answer, refer to both texts and try to use the collocations in bold in your answers.

1 How is their approach to shopping different?
2 Does Ben like spending?
3 What happened when they went shopping for a **big-ticket item**?
4 Why, according to Sue, was this a **false economy**?

Sue

Yes, I think I'm good with money. I'm certainly not extravagant, though I always consider the quality of a product as well as the price. Now, Ben – and please don't tell him I said this – is just mean. He doesn't like **parting with** his **cash**. To be honest, I think his attitude is often counter-productive. Last year, we had a huge argument about which washing machine to buy. He said the one I wanted **cost a fortune**, so we ended up buying a **dirt cheap** one. We've had that machine just eighteen months and we've already **spent a fortune** getting it repaired. Ben would say he was being economical, but to my mind that's **false economy**. With him, it's all about the price. Quality doesn't enter into it!

Ben

I'm definitely good with money – not mean, but I am careful. For example, if I want to buy a **big-ticket item**, I'll shop around until I find a good deal. The web is a great place for **bargain hunting**. I want **value for money** and that's fair enough, isn't it? After all, this is my **hard-earned** cash and I want to keep hold of it. Now, Sue is the complete opposite. She has what you'd call **expensive tastes**. When we went shopping for a new washing machine, she was happy to **pay over the odds** for something with a famous name on it. It's all about brands with her.

13.1

Leaving home

LEVEL
Elementary /
Pre-intermediate

ACTIVITY TYPE
Gap fill sentences
Discussion
Word forks

MATERIALS
One copy of the
worksheet for each
student

**TARGET
COLLOCATIONS**
do the housework,
feel homesick,
get home,
house-warming
party,
leave home,
live next door,
live on your own,
move house,
rent a house,
share a house

TIME
35–45 minutes

Warmer

Ask the students to tell the person sitting next to them where they live now and where they lived before their present address.

Input

1   Give each student a copy of the worksheet, folded as indicated. Ask the students to fill in the gaps in the text (Part A).
2   When they have finished, ask students to compare answers with a partner.
3   Check answers.

> **Answer key**
> **1** home **2** homesick **3** housework **4** rent **5** sharing **6** live **7** get
> **8** next door **9** moved **10** party

Practice

1   Ask students to fold over their pieces of paper so that they can only see the questions in Part B.
2   Explain that, for each question, they should underline the correct word.
3   When they have finished, ask them to compare answers with a partner.
4   Check answers.
5   Ask the students in pairs to take it in turn to ask each other the questions.

> **Answer key**
> **1** house **2** door **3** home **4** housework **5** party **6** home **7** felt
> **8** a house **9** house **10** live

Follow-up

1   Ask students to record the collocations they have learned in the word forks (Part C of their worksheet).
2   As a class, discuss any other collocations related to living and home. Students can record these on their worksheets.

● See page 125–6 for the best games from the CD-ROM to play after this unit.

A Complete the gaps with the words from the box:

rent	get	party	home	homesick	moved	housework	sharing	live	next door

Carla's new home

I left (1) .... at 18 to go to university. At first I felt very (2) .... away from my parents and I didn't like cooking for myself and **doing the** (3) .... I soon made friends with people from my course and started to enjoy myself. Now I (4) .... **a house** with friends in the city centre. I love (5) .... **a house** – I never want to (6) .... **on** my **own**. When I (7) .... **home** in the evening, I can chat with my housemates and we all cook dinner and eat together. Other students from my course **live** (8) .... too, so I'm never lonely. Before, I was living near the university with two girls but it was very expensive, so we (9) .... **house** to this place. We had a brilliant **house–warming** (10) .... and invited lots of people.

fold

B Choose the correct word(s) in italics in each sentence, and then ask your partner the questions.

1 When did you last move *house / home*?
2 Who lives next *door / house* to you?
3 At what age do children usually leave *house / home* in your country?
4 Who does the *homework / housework*, such as the cleaning and the ironing, in your house?
5 Have you ever had a house-warming *party / night*?
6 What time do you get *house / home* from work or school?
7 Have you ever *felt / had* homesick?
8 Have you ever shared *a house / house* with friends?
9 Would you prefer to buy or rent a *home / house*?
10 Would you like to *stay / live* on your own?

C Now record the collocations you have learned here:

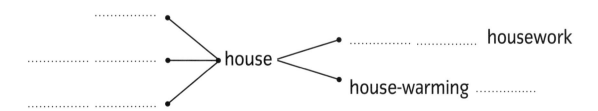

13.2

LEVEL
Intermediate

ACTIVITY TYPE
Matching collocations and definitions
Matching texts
Writing advertisements

MATERIALS
One copy of the worksheet for each student

TARGET COLLOCATIONS
block of flats, fitted kitchen, friendly neighbourhood, fully furnished, nicely furnished, off-street parking, overlook garden, residential area, shared house, spacious room, studio flat, within walking distance of (the station, etc.)

TIME
40–50 minutes

Room to let

Warmer

1 Elicit or teach the word *accommodation*.

2 Ask the students to write down three of four things that would be important to them if they were choosing accommodation.

3 Discuss ideas together as a class.

Input

1 Elicit or teach *to rent* and *to let* and *letting agent*.

2 Give each student a copy of the worksheet. Ask them to find phrases in the advertisements (Part A) that mean the same as the definitions and to underline those phrases.

3 Ask students to compare their answers with a partner.

4 Check answers.

> **Answer key**
> **1** friendly neighbourhood **2** overlooks the garden **3** shared house
> **4** off-street parking **5** studio flat **6** fitted kitchen **7** nicely furnished
> **8** block of flats **9** spacious rooms **10** within walking distance of
> **11** fully furnished **12** residential area

Practice

1 Put students in pairs. Refer them to the accommodation requirements task (Part B). Ask them to work together to find the most suitable accommodation for all three people. (Note that different answers are possible here. Students should discuss and justify their answers.)

2 Conduct feedback and try to agree as a class.

3 Ask the students to imagine that they are going to live in one of these three places and ask them to decide (on their own) their order of preference, i.e. first choice, second choice, third choice.

4 Then ask the students to explain their order of preference to a partner.

Follow-up

Ask the students to write an advertisement for a flat or house that they would like to live in.

See page 125–6 for the best games from the CD-ROM to play after this unit.

A Look at the advertisements below. Find collocations which mean ...

1   a nice area to live in because the people there are pleasant to each other
2   has a view of a garden
3   a house that two or more people live in
4   an area where a car can be parked that is not on a road
5   a flat with one room for sleeping and living in, a kitchen and a bathroom
6   a kitchen in which the cupboards, etc. are fixed to the wall
7   with attractive furniture
8   a large building divided into apartments.
9   large rooms
10 it is possible to walk easily to
11 with all the furniture that is needed
12 a place where most of the buildings are houses and flats, not offices or shops

Rooms to let

2 spacious rooms to rent (1 room which overlooks the garden) in beautifully modernised unfurnished shared house. In popular location, within walking distance of railway station. Professionals only to apply, please.

Room to let

1 small room available to rent in fully furnished flat, all modern appliances. Friendly neighbourhood, off-street parking. No garden, local park opposite. Available from Dec 1. Non-smokers only.

Studio flat to let

1 unfurnished studio flat to rent in newly built block of flats. Within walking distance of railway station, and close to local shops.

House to let

Small nicely furnished house to rent (2 bedrooms) in residential area. Modern fitted kitchen, large sitting room overlooking a small, attractive garden. Good local shops. No pets, please.

B Accommodation requirements

Now have a look at these notes made by a letting agent about the requirements of three of their clients. Which accommodation would you recommend for each person?

Julia
- Commutes to London by train
- Doesn't own a car
- Doesn't own any furniture
- Sociable

Dan
- Owns a car
- Owns a lot of furniture
- Likes being outdoors
- Not very interested in the appearance of his home

Raquel
- Uses the train a lot to visit friends
- Loves to cook
- Owns a car
- Likes her home to be attractive

13.3

A better place to live

LEVEL
Advanced

ACTIVITY TYPE
Reading
Role play
Preparing a report

MATERIALS
One copy of the
worksheet for each
student

**TARGET
COLLOCATIONS**
affordable housing,
antisocial behaviour,
deprived area,
due for demolition,
housing stock,
human habitation,
inner-city area,
littered pavements,
local amenities,
low-income families,
recycling facilities,
sense of community,
underage drinking

TIME
45 minutes – 1 hour

Warmer

Put students in pairs. Ask them to think of the three things that make an area good to live in, and three things that can cause problems in a residential area.

Input

1   Give each student a copy of the worksheet. Tell them this is a report about the problems associated with a poor area of a city and also a recommendation on how to deal with those problems. Ask the students to replace the phrases in italics with the appropriate collocations from the list.

2   Ask students to compare their answers with a partner.

3   Check answers.

> **Answer key**
> **1** deprived area   **2** inner-city areas   **3** human habitation   **4** due for demolition
> **5** antisocial behaviour   **6** underage drinking   **7** littered pavement
> **8** housing stock   **9** affordable housing   **10** low-income families
> **11** local amenities   **12** sense of community   **13** recycling facilities

Practice

1   Tell the class that they are going to attend a public meeting at which plans to develop an inner-city area are being discussed. Each of them must express their opinion as persuasively as possible to the rest of their group. Each person will have two minutes to explain their point of view and then there will be a general discussion. After the general discussion, each group will vote.

2   Give each student a role card (Part B) which tells them what stance they are to take. Allow ten minutes for them to make notes about what they are going to say at the meeting. Students should expand the points outlined in the role cards and think of other points that are relevant to their issues.

3   After ten minutes, put the students into groups of six. (For smaller groups, give students two role cards each.) Ask the students to start the meeting, presenting their points of view to the group.

4   Allow about 20 minutes for the meetings. After the meeting, each group votes for the three steps they would like to see taken, but they are *not* allowed to vote for their own suggestions!

Follow-up

Each group writes a report, based on their meeting, explaining what they have decided to do to improve their area. In the report they should also justify their decisions.

● See page 125–6 for the best games from the CD-ROM to play after this unit.

A Replace the phrases in italics in the report with collocations from the list in the box.

> affordable housing, antisocial behaviour, deprived area, due for demolition, housing stock, human habitation, inner-city area, littered pavements, local amenities, low-income families, recycling facilities, sense of community, underage drinking

Urban development report

This is generally a very (1) *poor area*. In common with other relatively poor (2) *areas near the city centre*, much of the housing is substandard. A large number (approximately 25%) of homes in the area are unoccupied, having been declared unfit for (3) *people to live in*. At least half of these are (4) *going to be pulled down*. Residents report a very poor quality of life, many complaining of (5) *actions that are harmful to the community*, especially among the area's youth. Much of this behaviour is attributed by police to (6) *the drinking of beer, wine, etc. by young people*. The area appears very run down, with graffiti and (7) *paths covered with paper, etc.* the norm. This is an area badly in need of redevelopment.

Broadly speaking, these are our recommendations for the regeneration of this area. The priority must be the replacement of the old and inadequate (8) *supply of houses* with good-quality (9) *houses that are not expensive*, suitable for (10) *families who don't receive much money*. Priority must also be given to the establishment of (11) *things such as community centres, green areas and swimming pools that improve life for people in the area* that will help to foster a (12) *feeling of loyalty to the people that you live near* in the area. Better and more visible (13) *equipment for collecting bottles, paper, etc. so that it can be used again* must also be provided to deal with the litter problem.

B Role cards

You want more affordable housing.
You are concerned that property prices are too high for the majority of low-earning people in this **deprived area**. You want to see more **affordable housing** for **low-income families**.

Your want better policing.
You believe that **antisocial behaviour** among young people is the biggest problem in the area. You also think that **underage drinking** is making the problem worse. You want to see better, more visible policing in the area to deal with the problem.

You want a better sense of community.
You believe that the key to success in any residential area is the way that people relate to each other. You would like to see improvements that will foster a **sense of community.** You want more **local amenities** that will bring people together, such as community centres, parks and swimming pools.

You want better housing stock.
You want to see the quality of the **housing stock** improved. You are convinced that the majority of the houses and flats in the area are unfit for **human habitation** and are to blame for many of the problems in this area. You think they are **due for demolition** and should be replaced.

You want a better environment.
You believe passionately that people need a pleasant environment to live in. You strongly believe that **littered pavements** and graffiti will be a thing of the past if more money is spent establishing green spaces and flowerbeds. You also want better **recycling facilities**.

LEVEL
Elementary /
Pre-intermediate

ACTIVITY TYPE
Jigsaw reading
Writing crime stories

MATERIALS
One copy of the
comprehension
questions for each
student
One copy of
worksheet Text A for
half the pairs, and a
copy of Text B for
the other half

**TARGET
COLLOCATIONS**
a serious crime,
call the police,
commit a crime,
go to prison,
pay a fine,
police arrest
someone,
rob a bank,
spend *x* years/
months in prison,
steal a bike,
steal a car

TIME
45 minutes

Call the police!

Warmer

Elicit some examples of crime, such as *stealing* and *murder*, and write them on the board.

Input

1   Explain to the students that they are going to read about a crime. Give each student a copy of the comprehension questions. Ask them to read them and make sure everyone understands them.

2   Have students work individually. Give half of them Text A and the other half Text B. Ask them to read their text, taking note of the collocations in bold, and to answer the comprehension questions for their text.

3   Put students in pairs with someone who read the same text. Ask them to compare answers and make any necessary changes to their answers. Conduct feedback to make sure students all have the right answers.

Answer key

	Text A	Text B
1	She stole a car.	He robbed a bank.
2	In June this year	Last December
3	Yes, the neighbour	It doesn't say.
4	Later the same day	Minutes later
5	Because it was a serious crime	Because it was a serious crime
6	Three months	Five years
7	No, although she paid a fine of £500 for a different crime (stealing a bike).	No

Practice

1   Put the students in new pairs so that each student who read Text A is with a partner who read Text B.

2   Ask the students to ask each other the comprehension questions to find out what happened in the other story and note down their partner's answers. Students should answer the questions without looking at their answers or the story.

3   Check answers as a whole group and write the answers on the board.

Follow-up

Ask the students in pairs to write their own crime stories, using the questions as guidelines. They should try to use the collocations in bold on their text paper (A or B).

See page 125–6 for the best games from the CD-ROM to play after this unit.

Text A

Woman sent to prison for stealing car

A woman **went to prison** yesterday for **stealing** her neighbour's **car**. The woman, Kelly White, aged 26, **committed** the **crime** in June of this year. Her neighbour **called the police** when she saw that her car had gone. Kelly White had stolen the car keys when she visited her neighbour that morning. **Police arrested** White later the same day. The judge said that stealing a car was a **serious crime** and that White must **spend** three **months in prison.** In January of this year, White was ordered to **pay** a **fine** of £500 for **stealing** a **bike** from another neighbour.

Text B

5 Years for robbing bank

A man **went to prison** yesterday for **robbing a bank**. The man, Lee Palmer, 29, **committed** the **crime** in December of last year, stealing over £30,000 in notes from the Melwich branch of the Bank of Union. Minutes later, **police arrested** him after his van crashed into a garage wall as he was leaving the village. The judge said that for such a **serious crime** Palmer must **spend** at least five years **in prison.**

Comprehension questions

Answer the questions below about the text you have read.

My answers   **My partner's answers**

- 1 What **crime** did he/she **commit**?   •

- 2 When did he/she **commit** the **crime**?   •

- 3 Did anyone **call** the **police**?   •

- 4 When did the **police arrest** him/her?   •

- 5 Why did he/she **go to prison**?   •

- 6 How long does he/she have to **spend in prison**? •

- 7 Does he/she have to **pay a fine**?   •

14.2

LEVEL
Intermediate

ACTIVITY TYPE
Gap fill
Running dictation
Writing
Discussion and
role play

MATERIALS
One copy of the gap
fill (Part A of the
worksheet) for each
student
One copy of the text
and comprehension
questions (Part B)
for each student
One set of six crime
cards (Part C), cut up,
for the class

**TARGET
COLLOCATIONS**
be found guilty,
be guilty of a crime,
be on the scene,
be sentenced to *x* years
in prison,
be severely punished,
begin a prison sentence,
break into a house,
criminal record,
plead guilty,
reach a verdict,
report *something/
someone* to the police,
serve a sentence

TIME
45 minutes – 1 hour

We have reached a verdict ...

Warmer

Tell the class that you are going to be talking about crime and punishment in this lesson. Write the word *sentence* on the board. Elicit the meaning and talk about the idea of a punishment involving staying in prison for a period of time.

Input

1 Give each student a copy of the gap fill sentences (Part A of the worksheet) and ask them to complete the gaps.

2 Ask students to compare their answers with a partner.

3 Check answers and write the collocations on the board.

> **Answer key**
>
> **1** prison **2** guilty **3** criminal **4** guilty **5** years **6** reach **7** police
> **8** scene **9** crime **10** severely **11** sentence

Practice

1 Put students in pairs. Show the class a copy of the newspaper report and comprehension questions (Part B). Tell them that the report is about a man who has committed a crime. Explain that they are going to copy the newspaper report, but that instead of giving it to them you are going to pin it up on the wall. Explain that *one* member of each pair should come and read *one* line of the text, then he/she should go back and tell that line to their partner, who will write it down. They should continue like this, line by line, until their partner has written down the whole of the first paragraph. Then the pair should swap roles for the second paragraph.

2 When each pair has finished, give each pair a copy of Part B. They should check their written-down text against the original and then answer the comprehension questions together.

3 Give out the remaining copies of Part B so that each student has a copy. Check answers (see below).

4 Ask the pairs to write their own account of a crime. To do this, they should look again at the comprehension questions and use them to structure their account.

> **Answer key**
>
> **1** burglary **2** Yes, he had a criminal record **3** Yes, he pleaded guilty **4** one year, three months **5** No – it only took them 30 minutes to reach a verdict
> **6** The neighbours reported it to the police **7** Yes, the police were on the scene within three minutes **8** No, he thinks he should serve his full sentence

Follow-up

1 Put the class into six groups (preferably of about 4–5 students each). Give each group one crime card (Part C). Explain that each group is now a jury and must discuss and agree on an appropriate punishment for the crime described on their card.

2 Ask each jury to elect a spokesperson to report back. They do so using collocations that they have learned, such as *We have reached a verdict of ... / We find x guilty of ... He/She will be sentenced to...*, etc.

3 The *juries'* swap cards and proceed as before with the new cards. (Each time this happens, a new spokesperson is elected.)

See page 125–6 for the best games from the CD-ROM to play after this unit.

A Complete the gaps in the sentences with the words in the box.

criminal	severely	prison	guilty	years	reach	sentence	police	scene	guilty	crime

1   A doctor **begins a** .... **sentence** today for the murder of his ex-wife.
2   At the end of the trial, she was **found** .... of murder.
3   Aged just 18, he already had a .... **record,** after committing several robberies as a teenager.
4   Both of the students admitted that they were in the wrong and **pleaded** .... to the crime they were accused of.
5   After the verdict, she was **sentenced to** five .... **in prison**.
6   At the end of a long and difficult trial, it took the jury 14 hours to .... **a verdict**.
7   I saw a man climbing over the wall and **reported** him **to the** ....
8   I called the police and they were **on the** .... within five minutes.
9   The sad truth is that she is **guilty of** a terrible ....
10 If she is found guilty she will be .... **punished**.
11 He is in prison, where he is **serving** a three-year .... for burglary.

✂ -

B

Guilty verdict

A 31-year-old man is **beginning a prison sentence** after being **found guilty** of burglary in Warwickshire. Karl O'Neil, who already has a **criminal record**, was sentenced at Warwick Crown Court after **pleading guilty** to committing the burglary. He was **sentenced to** one **year** and three months in prison. It took the jury just thirty minutes to **reach** the **verdict** of guilty.

Neighbours saw the man climbing out of the ground-floor window of a house just after midnight on April 22 and immediately **reported** the incident **to the police**. The police were **on the scene** within three minutes. "Burglary is a very serious crime which often leaves the victims terrified," the judge said. "People who are **guilty of** this type of **crime** must be **severely punished**. I strongly recommend that O'Neil **serve** the full **sentence**."

Answer the questions.

1   What crime did he commit?
2   Had he committed a crime before?
3   Did he admit that he was responsible for the burglary?
4   How long was his prison sentence?
5   Do you think the jury found it difficult to make a decision? Why / why not?
6   Who called the police?
7   Did the police arrive quickly?
8   Does the judge think O'Neil should be let out of prison early?

✂ -

C Crime cards

Two young men break into and burgle an elderly couple's house.	A woman's dog attacks and severely injures a small child in the street.
A man robs a couple in the street, taking the man's phone and his MP3 player. The woman is unhurt.	A 13-year-old robs a woman in the street, taking her mobile phone and punching her in the face.
A man burgles a house six months after burgling another house.	A woman steals her sister's car keys and takes her car.

14.3

Does the punishment fit the crime?

LEVEL
Advanced

ACTIVITY TYPE
Writing two
opposing texts
Role play

MATERIALS
One copy of the
worksheet for each
student

**TARGET
COLLOCATIONS**
act as a deterrent,
behind bars,
carry a sentence,
condone *someone's*
actions,
extenuating
circumstances,
get off lightly,
hardened criminal,
hefty sentence,
law-abiding citizen,
lenient sentence,
previous
convictions,
show remorse,
stiff penalty,
unprovoked attack

TIME
45 minutes

Warmer

Ask students if they can think of any examples where a court has given a sentence that they did not agree with. Use a recent example from the news if appropriate.

Input

1 Give each student a copy of the worksheet.

2 Refer students to Text A. Ask them to read it and decide if they think the sentence was fair.

3 Ask students to compare their ideas with a partner.

4 Now refer students to the responses (A and B) of the two members of the public.

5 Ask students in their pairs to discuss which response they agree with more and feed back the opinions as a class.

6 Ask the pairs to write the numbers 1–14 down one side of a sheet of paper. Read out the definitions (from the answer key below) in turn, and ask students to identify which of the collocations in bold in the two responses (A and B) each definition refers to. Allow students enough time between each definition to discuss their answers, and write them down.

> **Answer key**
>
> 1 to not be punished severely for something bad that you have done: *get off lightly*
>
> 2 a punishment that is not severe given by a judge: *lenient sentence*
>
> 3 to usually result in a particular punishment: *carry a sentence*
>
> 4 in prison: *behind bars*
>
> 5 to discourage someone from doing something because they are afraid of what will happen if they do it: *act as a deterrent*
>
> 6 to accept or allow someone's bad behaviour: *condone someone's actions*
>
> 7 a severe punishment: *hefty sentence*
>
> 8 a situation which causes a wrong act to be punished less severely: *extenuating circumstances*
>
> 9 when someone is physically violent towards a person who has done nothing to deserve it: *unprovoked attack*
>
> 10 a person who has committed so many crimes that they are not now emotionally affected by their actions: *hardened criminal*
>
> 11 crimes that someone has been found guilty of in the past: *previous convictions*
>
> 12 a person who always obeys the law: *law-abiding citizen*
>
> 13 to show that you are very sorry about something that you have done: *show remorse*
>
> 14 a severe punishment: *stiff penalty*

Practice

1 Keep students in the same pairs and refer them to Text B.

2 Ask them to use the questions to prepare in note form two opposing responses to the crime and its punishment. Explain that they should use the collocations that they have just learned and any other language they know relating to crime and punishment.

3 Form new groups of four. In each group make one pair A and one pair B. Ask each pair to discuss the crime, with each student in the pair taking an opposing viewpoint.

4 Now switch the pairs around within the groups so that each student is working with a different person and taking an opposing viewpoint to the one they took before.

Follow-up

1 Hold a whole-class discussion based around Text B.

➤ See page 125–6 for the best games from the CD-ROM to play after this unit.

Read Text A below. Do you think the ten-year sentence was fair?

Text A

Mr X is serving a prison sentence for murdering his neighbour. Over a period of a year, he had repeatedly complained to his neighbour about unacceptable noise levels after the neighbour held a series of all-night parties. In addition, the neighbour had three large dogs which barked throughout the night. The neighbour refused to silence his dogs and persisted with his parties. Mr X reported his neighbour's behaviour to the police but they did nothing. One night when his neighbour was holding a particularly noisy party, Mr X went to see him. The neighbour refused to turn his music down. In a fit of fury, Mr X punched the neighbour hard. The neighbour fell, hitting his head as he did so. He later died of a head injury. Mr X was devastated. He has been convicted of murder and sentenced to ten years in prison.

Response A

'I think he **got off lightly**. Ten years in prison for killing a bloke? That was a **lenient sentence** – too lenient, in my opinion. Yes he was provoked and I know he'd complained to the police and they'd done nothing, but still, that doesn't excuse what he did. Anyone who resorts to violence in this sort of situation must be a pretty nasty individual. If it was up to me, murder would **carry a** minimum **sentence** of twenty years. Someone who intentionally kills another person should, for the good of society, spend most of their life **behind bars**. It's a very serious offence, whichever way you look at it. In some countries this man would be put to death for this crime. Now I'm not saying that I personally believe in capital punishment. On the other hand, the death sentence almost certainly **acts as a deterrent** whereas a ten-year sentence certainly wouldn't.'

Response B

'The sentencing seems to me rather harsh. Of course this man has committed a very serious offence – I don't for a moment **condone** his **actions**. No one should take another person's life. But this is a very **hefty sentence** given the neighbour's behaviour. Didn't the jury consider these **extenuating circumstances**? This wasn't an **unprovoked attack**. And of course, he didn't mean to kill the man. He must have punched him pretty hard to have caused his death but it wasn't his intention to kill him. I'm assuming from what I've heard of the case that this man wasn't a **hardened criminal** – he had no **previous convictions** for violent crime. If this is true and he was a **law-abiding citizen** who was provoked and who has now **shown remorse**, then I think this is an inappropriately **stiff penalty**.'

Now read Text B. Use the questions below to prepare (in note form) two opposing viewpoints of this crime and its punishment.

Text B

A man was in a nightclub with his friends. A stranger approached the group and started insulting one of the man's friends. The man got angry and told the stranger to leave his friend alone He was verbally aggressive but not physically aggressive to the stranger. The stranger walked away but, half an hour later, came back and threatened the man with a knife. There was a fight during which the man took the knife from the stranger and stabbed him. The stranger later died from a single stab wound. The man had no previous convictions for violent crime. He was described by friends and colleagues alike as 'a good and decent man' and 'someone who wouldn't hurt a fly'. Three months after the attack he is still in a state of shock over what he has done. He is serving a 15-year prison sentence for murder.

Questions

1 Was this an **unprovoked attack**?

2 Were there any **extenuating circumstances**?

3 Prior to the crime, was this man a **law-abiding citizen**?

4 Does the man **show** any **remorse**?

5 Is this a **lenient sentence** given the circumstances, or a **hefty sentence**?

6 Should we in any way **condone** his **actions**?

7 Do you think sentences like this **act as a deterrent**?

8 What **sentence** do you think this crime should **carry**?

15.1

Home computer

LEVEL
Elementary /
Pre-intermediate

ACTIVITY TYPE
Gap fill
Class survey

MATERIALS
One copy of the
worksheet for each
student

**TARGET
COLLOCATIONS**
check your email,
copy text,
create a new
document,
do a search,
go online,
lose your work,
new message,
online shopping,
save a document,
send an email,
start up a computer,
visit a website

TIME
40–50 minutes

Warmer

1 Discuss with students whether they use a computer at home and if so what they use a computer for.

2 Ensure that some of the concepts/collocations come up during the discussion and are written on the board, just to get the students started.

Input

1 Put students in pairs. Give each pair a copy of the worksheet and focus the students on the collocations in the box in Part A. Make sure they understand what they all mean.

2 Ask students to write the collocations in the correct place in the three short texts.

3 Give out the remaining copies of the worksheet so that each student has a copy. Check answers.

> ### Answer key
> 1 started up the computer   2 check my email   3 sent an email
> 4 new messages   5 go online   6 online shopping   7 visit websites
> 8 did a search 9 created a new document   10 copy text   11 save the document
> 12 lost all my work

Practice

1 Refer students to the class survey (Part B).

2 Have students work individually, going through each question and making sure that they know what the missing collocation is. (They can refer back to the texts but they should not write the collocations in.)

> ### Answer key
> 1 online shopping   2 new messages   3 save your documents
> 4 start up your computer   5 copy your emails   6 done a search   7 copy text
> 8 create a new document   9 go online   10 lost your work   11 visited a website
> 12 sent an email

3 Have students mingle, asking each other the questions in turn. They should finish the exercise with a different name next to every question, so when a student answers 'yes' to a question, they should write it down and move on to the next student.

Follow-up

Ask students to write some interview questions for someone they know who uses a computer a lot. They should interview that person and write a short summary of their findings.

See page 125–6 for the best games from the CD-ROM to play after this unit.

A Collocations

started up the computer new messages copy text visit websites sent an email lost all my work online shopping check my email save the document created a new document did a search go online	

Three people are talking about their experiences with computers. Read what they say and put the collocations from the box above in the correct places.

When I (1) .... this morning, the first thing I did was (2) ....
Yesterday I (3) .... to Suki, inviting her to the cinema, and I wanted to see her reply. There were eleven (4) .... in my inbox, but nothing from Suki.

I (5) .... nearly every day, and that is why I never have any money – I spend it all on (6) .... I especially like to (7) .... about food and cooking. You can find anything on the Internet – once I (8) .... for 'animal cake tins' and I found tins in the shape of every animal, from bears to elephants.

I had to write an essay about global warming, so first I (9) .... Our teacher said we could look for information on the Internet, but we were not allowed to (10) .... from websites.
After writing for two hours, I went for a cup of coffee, but unfortunately I forgot to (11) ....
When I came back, I discovered that my little brother had switched the computer off and I had (12) ....

✂ --

B Class survey

Questions	Name
1 Have you done any o............... s............... in the last week?	
2 Do you usually get more than 10 n............... m............... a day?	
3 Do you always remember to s............... your d............... at least every 15 minutes?	
4 Did you s............... u......... your c............... before 8 a.m. yesterday?	
5 Do you c............... your e............... more than three times a day?	
6 Have you d............... a s............... for your own name on the Internet?	
7 Do you think it is wrong to c............... t............... from the Internet to use in an essay?	
8 Do you c............... a n............... d............... every day?	
9 Do you g............... o............... most days?	
10 Have you ever l............... your w............... because something went wrong with your computer?	
11 Have you ever v............... a w............... to look for cheap flights or a cheap holiday?	
12 Have you ever s............... an e............... which you were sorry about later?	

15.2

LEVEL
Intermediate

ACTIVITY TYPE
Writing definitions
Role play

MATERIALS
One copy of the lists
(Part A of the
worksheet) for each
student
Six blank slips of
paper to write on for
each pair
One copy of the role
cards (Part B) cut up
for each pair

**TARGET
COLLOCATIONS**
a password expires,
an email bounces,
delete a file,
enter a password,
forward an email,
install software,
open an attachment,
print out a document,
read an attachment,
restart a computer,
run software,
shut down a
computer

TIME
45 minutes – 1 hour

Help – it won't work!

Warmer

Ask your class whether they think computers are a good thing. What are the advantages?
Are there any disadvantages?

Input

1   Put students in pairs. Give each pair Part A of the worksheet and ask half the pairs to look
    at the collocations in List 1, and the other half to look at the collocations in List 2. Also give
    each pair six blank slips of paper to write on.

2   Ask pairs to write a definition for each of the collocations in their list. Allow them to use
    dictionaries, but they should write the definitions in their own words. Circulate and check
    answers as students write.

3   When they have finished, ask students to swap their definitions and collocations with a
    pair who looked at the other list.

4   Each pair should now match the collocations to the definitions.

5   Conduct whole-class feedback, going through all the collocations, asking for definitions
    and checking that all the collocations have been correctly understood. Make sure all the
    students have a record of all the collocations and their definitions.

Practice

1   Give each pair a set of role cards (Part B of the worksheet).

2   Ask pairs to match each user card to the appropriate helpdesk card.

3   Check answers (see worksheet).

Follow-up

1   Place several complete sets of user and helpdesk cards around the room (one set for each
    pair of students).

2   Ask each pair to go and stand near a set of cards.

3   Explain that they should role play the situations on the cards. Explain that the user
    (Student A) should begin the conversation, and the helpdesk (Student B) should respond.
    Both students should wait to give the information in brackets until later in the
    conversation.

4   When pairs finish a dialogue, they should move to another set of cards and role play them.

5   Continue for as long as is appropriate. At the end conduct whole-class feedback.

⬤ See page 125–6 for the best games from the CD-ROM to play after this unit.

A

List 1	**List 2**
• open an attachment	• read an attachment
• enter a password	• a password expires
• print out a document	• run software
• install software	• shut down a computer
• restart a computer	• an email bounces
• forward an email	• delete a file

B Role cards

User	**Helpdesk**
You can't **open the attachment** that a client has sent you. (You are very worried because your boss has told you to deal with it today.)	Suggest they try saving the file on their hard disk and opening it from there. (Explain that they should always be careful about opening attachments in case they contain a virus.)
User	**Helpdesk**
You've **entered your password**, but the system won't let you in. (You are angry because this has happened several times before.)	Ask them if they've got 'Caps Lock' pressed down. (If they haven't, tell them that their **password has** probably **expired**. Offer to help them set up a new password.)
User	**Helpdesk**
You've accidentally **deleted a file** with all the company's sales figures on it. (You are very embarrassed.)	Tell them not to worry because it should still be in their 'trash' folder. (Ask them to look there and see if they can find it.)
User	**Helpdesk**
You're trying to contact a customer, Sarah Green, but your **email bounced**. (You are worried that her company has gone out of business.)	Ask them if they have used that address successfully recently. (Suggest they search for her company on the Internet to see if they can find any information about it.)
User	**Helpdesk**
You're trying to **print out a document** but the symbols have come out all wrong. (You really need the document immediately for a meeting.)	Tell them that you'll need to **install some software** that will allow them to print these symbols correctly. (Tell them that you are really busy and you can't do it until tomorrow.)
User	**Helpdesk**
You **forwarded an email** to your colleague, Joe, but he can't **read the attachment**. (You think it's probably Joe's fault because he's very bad at using computers.)	Suggest they try copying the text of the attachment into the email itself. (Explain that an error in Joe's computer may be causing the problem.)
User	**Helpdesk**
You **ran** some new **software** and since then nothing seems to work properly. (You apologise to the helpdesk, because this is the third time you've called them today.)	Ask them if they have tried **restarting their computer**. (Ask them where they got the software from. Tell them that they should check with you before **installing** any new **software** on a company computer.)
User	**Helpdesk**
Your computer is giving off a terrible smell, and it's hot to touch. (You are very anxious as you think you might set the office on fire.)	Tell them to **shut down their computer** immediately and unplug it. (Say that you will call an engineer immediately.)

15.3

What do you use *yours* for?

LEVEL
Advanced

ACTIVITY TYPE
Categorising
Definitions game

MATERIALS
One set of three
pictures and the
collocations (Part A)
One copy of the
three texts (Part B)
Dictionaries
Two or three cards
per students (Part
C). Make sure that at
least one complete
set is given out

**TARGET
COLLOCATIONS**
archive your
documents,
back up your work,
bookmark a site,
create an avatar,
debug a program,
download a podcast,
download music,
format a document,
install an application,
make a hard copy,
navigate a website,
position the cursor,
resize a window,
write code,
zip/unzip a file

TIME
45 minutes – 1 hour

Warmer

1 Write the words *navigate* and *website* as anagrams on the board. Give students the clue *Internet* if they find the anagrams difficult to solve.

2 Repeat the game using anagrams for *site*, *bookmark*, *podcast* and *download*.

3 Make sure students understand these words within the context of computers and the Internet.

Input

1 Put students in pairs and give each pair a copy of Part A of the worksheet.

2 Ask each pair to look at the collocations and read about the three people. They should then match the collocations to the people. (Some collocations could be done by more than one person.) Allow students to use a dictionary if necessary.

3 Conduct feedback, asking pairs to justify their answers, and make sure everyone understands the collocations.

> **Answer key**
> **Suggested answers:**
> - archive your documents: P, L, and J
> - back up your work: P, L, and J
> - bookmark a site: L
> - create an avatar: L
> - debug a program: J
> - download music: J
> - download a podcast: L and J
> - format a document: P, L, and J
> - install an application: L and J
> - make a hard copy: P
> - navigate a website: L
> - position the cursor: P, L and J
> - resize a window: P, L, and J
> - write code: J
> - zip/unzip a file: P, L and J

Practice

1 Put students in groups of five or six and refer them to the three texts (Part B of the worksheet). Ask them to work out what words are missing from the gaps but not to write them in yet.

2 Give each student two or three words from Part C of the worksheet, making sure that all the word cards are given out randomly within the group.

3 Explain to the students that before they can write a word in a gap they have to find someone who has that word. To find a student with a word, they cannot simply ask for the word; they have to paraphrase it. For example, if they want the word *navigate*, they could say, *Have you got the word that means to move around a website?* When they find the person with the right word, they write the word in the appropriate gap, and the person's initials or name in the margin next to it.

4 Explain that each group can share the work between them so that one person in each group finds the words for one text. Each group can also work together to think of how to paraphrase the words.

5 When the groups have finished, check answers by asking for the words and the names of the people who had the words.

> **Answer key**
> 1 zipped 2 formatted 3 position 4 resize 5 hard copy 6 back up
> 7 archive 8 installed 9 code 10 debugging 11 bookmarked 12 podcast
> 13 avatars 14 download 15 navigate

Follow-up

1 Ask students to discuss which of the collocations they do themselves.

2 Ask them to put them in order, according to how often they do them, and to describe the things they find most difficult.

> ● See page 125–6 for the best games from the CD-ROM to play after this unit.

A

> archive your documents, back up your work, bookmark a site, create an avatar, debug a program, download music, format a document, install an application, make a hard copy, navigate a website, position the cursor, resize a window, download a podcast, write code, zip/unzip a file

Petra, 45, is an administrative assistant in a small transport company. She is responsible for keeping records of the company's orders and sending out customers' bills. She never uses a computer outside of work.

Lulu, 18, is a media studies student. She uses the Internet for studying, but also loves social networking.

Jan, 25, is a computer programmer. In his spare time, he loves listening to music.

B

Text 1

My friend Georg asked me if I would translate an article he had written in German about diseases of cereal crops, and I said yes. I must have been mad! When he emailed it to me, I found he'd (1) .... the file. This was really annoying because I didn't know how to unzip it. He'd (2) .... the document in a really weird way, too, so there were little lines and boxes all over the place. My heart really sank when I saw it. Luckily, I found some cool translation software on the web. All you have to do is (3) .... the cursor over the text and a translation pops up in a new window. You can (4) .... the window if it's too big. I made a (5) .... of the original document too because I like to refer to it when I work. Automatic translation isn't that accurate, but it was certainly better than starting from scratch!

Text 2

If it wasn't for me, our office would be in complete chaos! I just can't believe how disorganised my colleagues are. They don't (6) .... their work unless I remind them, and they always forget to (7) .... their documents, so they have enormous folders full of stuff from years ago that is no use to anyone and stops them finding what they need. I (8) .... an application to improve our accounting systems, but nobody bothers to use it. They say it's too complicated. But even worse than the people who don't understand the software are those who think they do. One chap assured me he could write (9) .... but I had to spend the rest of the week (10) .... his program.

Text 3

My mum is such a pain. She found out that I'd (11) .... a site about dieting, and now she won't shut up about it. She even downloaded a (12) .... about anorexia and made me listen to it. Like I could ever stop eating chocolate long enough to get that thin! I'm not unhappy with how I look, but my friends and I have all created (13) .... that are how we'd like to be in an ideal world. Mine is taller than me, and has long black hair (mine is short and mouse-coloured). As well as social networking, I often (14) .... music onto my MP3 player for the bus journey to school. Our school has just started putting all our homework online, which means my mum can see what I'm supposed to be doing. Luckily for me, though, it's quite hard to (15) .... the website, and I'm certainly not going to help her, so usually she just gives up.

C Word cards

back up	archive	installed	code	debugging
bookmarked	podcast	avatars	download	navigate
zip	formatted	position	resize	hard copy

16.1

Wish you were here!

LEVEL
Elementary /
Pre-intermediate

ACTIVITY TYPE
Matching
collocations
Gap fill sentences
Writing postcards

MATERIALS
One copy of the
pictures collocations
(Part A of the
worksheet) for each
student
One copy of the gap
fill sentences (Part
B) for each student
One copy of the
blank postcard
template (Part C) for
each student

**TARGET
COLLOCATIONS**
bright sunshine,
calm sea,
dark clouds,
heavy rain,
high mountains,
sandy beach,
snow falls,
steep hill,
strong winds,
thick fog

TIME
40–50 minutes

Warmer

Ask students where they like going on holiday. What is the weather like and what is the scenery like?

Input

1   Give each pair of students Part A of the worksheet.

2   Ask them to read through the collocations and match them to the pictures.

3   Check that everyone has the right answers

> **Answer key**
> **1** Sandy beach / bright sunshine   **2** high mountains / snow falls   **3** calm sea / thick fog   **4** steep hill / heavy rain   **5** strong winds / dark clouds

Practice

1   Give each student a copy of the gap fill sentences (Part B), and ask them to complete them with the collocations from Part A.

2   Ask students to compare answers with a partner.

3   Check answers.

> **Answer key**
> **1** high mountain / snow (was) falling   **2** sandy beach / bright sunshine   **3** calm sea / thick fog   **4** strong winds / dark clouds   **5** heavy rain / steep hill

4   Now ask students to match the sentences to the pictures, and draw what is described in the sentences onto the pictures.

Follow-up

Give each student a copy of the blank postcard (Part C). Ask students to choose one of the pictures and imagine they are on holiday there. They should write a postcard to a friend or family member.

See page 125–6 for the best games from the CD-ROM to play after this unit.

A Look at the pictures. Match them with the collocations in the box.

> bright sunshine, calm sea, dark clouds, heavy rain, high mountains, sandy beach, snow (was) falling, steep hill, strong winds, thick fog

✂ ---

B Now use the collocations to complete the gaps.

1 I climbed a really .... It was very cold and .... was ....

2 We go to the .... every day and make sandcastles in the lovely ....
   ....

3 We went out in a boat on the .... , but .... came in and we couldn't see anything at all!

4 I stayed in all day because the weather was awful. There were .... and the sky was full of ....

5 There was .... so I needed my umbrella to walk up the ....
   .... to school.

✂ ---

C

```
                                              To

                                              _____

                                              _____

                                              _____

                                              _____

                                              _____
```

From *Collocations Extra* by Elizabeth Walter and Kate Woodford © Cambridge University Press 2010 **PHOTOCOPIABLE** **103**

16.2

Disaster!

LEVEL
Intermediate

ACTIVITY TYPE
Reading
Running dictation
Writing

MATERIALS
One copy of the
three pictures and
the three newspaper
reports (Part A of
the worksheet) for
each pair
Two or three copies
of the comprehension
questions (Part B)
and something to
stick them on the wall

**TARGET
COLLOCATIONS**
boat capsizes,
bring chaos,
bring down cables,
cause damage,
experience
difficulties,
extreme weather
conditions,
icy waters,
radio for help,
rain heavily,
rivers burst their
banks,
rough sea,
struck by lightning,
towns are cut off,
violent storms,
widespread flooding

TIME
45 minutes – 1 hour

Warmer

Discuss bad weather and things that happen when it occurs.

Input

1   Give each student a copy of Part A of the worksheet.
2   Ask them to skim read the reports very quickly and decide which report goes with which picture.

> **Answer key**
> 1c, 2a, 3b

4   Then ask students to read the reports in more detail, underlining the words that form collocations with the words in the boxes below them.
5   Check answers, making sure that all the collocations are understood.

> **Answer key**
> 1   <u>violent</u> storms, <u>bringing down</u> electricity cables, <u>causing</u> damage, <u>struck by</u> lightning, <u>extreme</u> weather conditions
> 2   <u>widespread</u> flooding, <u>brought</u> chaos, rivers <u>burst their banks</u>, towns <u>are cut off</u>, rain <u>heavily</u>
> 3   boat <u>capsized</u>, <u>rough</u> sea, <u>radioed for</u> help, <u>experiencing</u> difficulties, <u>icy</u> waters

Practice

1   Put two or three copies of the comprehension questions (Part B) up on the walls (depending on how many students you have in your class).
2   Put students in pairs and explain that one student from each pair should run to the questions, memorise a question, then run back and tell it to their partner, who should write it down.
3   When the pair has all the comprehension questions written down, they should write down the answers to them all, using the collocations they have learned. Make a note of which pair finishes first. (If all the answers are correct, they will be the winners.)
4   Check answers.

> **Answer key**
> 1   Violent storms have brought down electricity cables.
> 2   It caused damage to millions of pounds' worth of property.
> 3   His roof was struck by lightning.
> 4   The extreme weather conditions could be connected to global warming.
> 5   Widespread flooding has brought chaos, after several rivers burst their banks.
> 6   Helicopters are bringing supplies to towns in Wales because they have been cut off by the floods.
> 7   No, the flooding isn't likely to get better because it is expected to rain again heavily.
> 8   The sailors are missing because their boat capsized in rough sea.
> 9   The sailors radioed for help because they started experiencing difficulties.
> 10 No, it is not likely that the sailors will be found alive because it is unlikely that they will survive in the icy waters.

Follow-up

Put students in new pairs. Ask them to write a government information leaflet about what to do in the event of extreme weather conditions.

🌐 See page 125–6 for the best games from the CD-ROM to play after this unit.

A Match the pictures to the text.

a

b

c

B Underline the words in the texts which form collocations with the words in the box.

1

Thousands of people today find themselves without power after violent storms battered the north of England overnight, bringing down electricity cables and causing damage to millions of pounds' worth of property. One homeowner in Hull described how he was in bed when his roof was struck by lightning. 'I thought a bomb had gone off,' he said. Scientists say these extreme weather conditions may be connected to global warming.

| storms | cables | damage |
| lightning | weather conditions | |

2

Widespread flooding, after several rivers burst their banks, has brought chaos to parts of Wales. Whole towns are cut off by the floods, and in some cases emergency supplies are being flown in by helicopter. Unfortunately, the worst may be still to come: meteorologists expect it to rain heavily again tonight.

| flooding | chaos | rivers | towns | rain |

3

Two sailors were missing yesterday after their boat capsized in rough sea off the coast of Scotland. The crew had radioed for help after experiencing difficulties. A search for the men continues, but it is unlikely they could survive for more than a few minutes in the icy waters.

| boat | sea | help | difficulties | waters |

✂ -

B Answer the questions

1 Why do of people in the north of England have no electricity?

2 How did this affect property in the area?

3 Why did the man in Hull think a bomb had gone off?

4 What did the scientists say about global warming?

5 What has brought chaos to Wales?

6 Why are helicopters bringing supplies to towns in Wales?

7 Is the flooding in Wales likely to get better soon?

8 Why are the sailors missing?

9 Why did the sailors radio for help?

10 Is it likely that the sailors will be found alive?

16.3

LEVEL
Advanced

ACTIVITY TYPE
Writing definitions
Jumbled texts
Writing journal
entries

MATERIALS
Five of the
collocation cards
(Part A of the
worksheet) for each
group (make sure
every collocation
card is given out to
at least one of the
groups)
Dictionaries
A copy of the three
texts (Part B) for
each student

**TARGET
COLLOCATIONS**
blanket of fog,
dense forest,
fast-flowing river,
fog lifts,
gusty winds,
hard frost,
heavy seas,
panoramic views,
rolling hills,
rugged mountains,
secluded beach,
stifling heat,
storm abates,
torrential rain,
tropical island

TIME
45 minutes – 1 hour

Adventure travel

Warmer

Discuss the idea of holiday travel and longer-term travel (e.g. *round-the-world trips, living in another country for a number of years, adventure travel*). Ask students to give their opinions and talk about their experiences.

Input

1 Put the class into groups of 4–6. Give each group five of the collocation cards.

2 Explain that each group should write definitions for their collocations on a sheet of paper. They can use dictionaries to help them but should rewrite any definitions they look up in the dictionary in their own words.

3 When they have finished, have each group pass their collocation cards and corresponding definitions to the next group, who should match the collocations to the definitions.

4 Have the groups pass the collocations and definitions on a final time.

5 When all the groups have seen all the collocations and definitions, go through them and make sure all the students have a record of the collocations and their correct meanings.

Answer key
Suggested definitions:
blanket of fog: a thick layer of fog, making it very difficult to see anything
dense forest: a forest where trees grow close together
fast-flowing rivers: rivers with a lot of water that flows very fast
fog lifts: fog goes away
gusty winds: winds that blow in short, strong bursts
hard frost: thick frost when the weather is very cold
heavy seas: sea that is very rough, with big waves
panoramic views: fantastic views over a very wide area
rolling hills: groups of hills with smooth gentle slopes
rugged mountains: mountains with uneven and sharply pointed tops
secluded beach: a quiet and sheltered beach, often with few people on it
stifling heat: heat that makes you feel as if you cannot breathe
storm abates: a storm gets less strong
torrential rain: extremely heavy rain
tropical island: an island in a hot part of the world close to the equator

Practice

1 Give each student a copy of the texts. Explain that they are all extracts from different travellers' journals. The collocations in them are mixed up.

2 Ask students to put the collocations back in the correct places (making necessary changes to the tense where appropriate).

3 Ask students to compare answers with a partner.

Answer key

1 heavy seas **2** torrential rain **3** storm abated **4** tropical island **5** dense forest **6** hard frost **7** gusty winds **8** blanket of fog **9** rolling hills **10** fog lifted **11** stifling heat **12** panoramic views **13** rugged mountains **14** fast-flowing rivers **15** secluded beaches

Follow-up

1 Ask students to write an entry from a journal, real or imaginary, about *a perfect day*, or *a nightmare day*. Encourage the students to be creative – they can include shark attacks, hidden treasure, plane crashes … anything!

2 Display the texts around the room so that everyone can read them.

See page 125–6 for the best games from the CD-ROM to play after this unit.

A Collocation cards

hard frost	fast-flowing river	stifling heat	blanket of fog	heavy seas
dense forest	secluded beach	gusty winds	panoramic views	a storm abates
rolling hills	tropical island	fog lifts	torrential rain	rugged mountains

B The collocations are mixed up. Put them back in the correct place.

Leonie:

We had been tossed around in (1) **hard frost** all night. I was soaking wet because (2) **fast-flowing rivers** had lashed the decks, but I felt so sick that I could not bear to be inside in the dry. I think my sickness saved my life because as soon as we hit the rocks, I understood what had happened and was able to jump into one of the lifeboats. Others, trapped in their cabins, were not so lucky. We made it to the shore, and when eventually the (3) **stifling heat** and the sun rose, we found ourselves on a small (4) **blanket of fog** covered in (5) **heavy seas**.

Peter:

Living in this beautiful countryside, I find it impossible to stay miserable for long. This morning, for instance, I was in a bad mood at breakfast, looking out of the window at my garden. A (6) **dense forest** the previous week had killed my tomato plants, and (7) **secluded beaches** had brought down branches from my fruit trees. After breakfast, I decided that I must at least go outside and make a start on clearing up. The valley below our cottage was shrouded in a (8) **gusty winds**, and the (9) **panoramic views** in the distance looked grey and threatening in the gloom. With a heavy heart, I lifted my garden fork. Just at that moment, a thrush began to sing and a shaft of sunlight broke through the clouds. Within an hour, the (10) **storm abated**, the valley below was glowing in the sunshine, and all was well in my world again.

Simone:

I stepped off the plane into the (11) **rolling hills** of the afternoon. A taxi took me to my hotel, which, perched on top of a hill, had (12) **tropical island** of the city and the (13) **fog had lifted** beyond, with their majestic, snow-capped peaks. During the next few days, I explored the area, picnicking by (14) **torrential rain** and sunbathing on (15) **rugged mountains**. It was the perfect holiday, and I soon got used to the heat.

What exercise do you do?

LEVEL
Elementary /
Pre-intermediate

ACTIVITY TYPE
Listening
Class survey

MATERIALS
One set of the
pictures (Part A of
the worksheet) for
each pair of
students, and one
single set cut up
into cards for the
whole class
One copy of the
word trees (Part B
of the worksheet)
for each student
One copy of the
Group 1 questions
(Part C) for half the class
and one copy of the
Group 2 questions for the
other half of the class
One frequency phrase for
each student (Part D)

**TARGET
COLLOCATIONS**
do aerobics,
do karate,
do sport/exercise,
do yoga ,
go jogging,
go riding,
go swimming,
go to the gym,
play football,
play golf,
play hockey,
play tennis

TIME
45 minutes – 1 hour

Warmer

1 Put students in pairs and give each pair a copy of the pictures (Part A of the worksheet).

2 Elicit/teach the words for each exercise and sport shown in the pictures: *karate, yoga, aerobics, football, tennis, hockey, golf, swimming, riding, jogging, gym.*

Input

1 Explain to the class that you are going to read out some sentences (in point 2 below) and they will need to listen carefully. Explain that they will not remember everything you are going to say, but they should try to remember three or four things. Explain that they cannot write anything down.

2 Read out these sentences:

- Sam does a lot of exercise.
- He does yoga every morning.
- He plays football once a week.
- He plays tennis once a week in the summer.
- He never plays hockey.
- He plays golf once a month.

- He goes swimming three times a week.
- He never goes riding.
- He goes jogging at the weekend.
- He never does karate.
- He never does aerobics.
- He goes to the gym twice a week in the winter.

3 Divide the class into two groups. Give one group the Group 1 questions (Part C of the worksheet) and give the other group the Group 2 questions. Ask students to work together to see if they can remember the answers to their set of questions.

4 Check answers.

5 Put students in pairs so that each pair consists of a student who answered the Group 1 questions and a student who answered the Group 2 questions. Give each pair Part B of the worksheet and ask them to write in the sports and types of exercise from the questions in the spaces provided.

> **Answer key**
> **play:** football, tennis, hockey, golf   **go:** swimming, riding, jogging, to the gym
> **do:** sport, karate, yoga, aerobics

Practice

1 Give each student a picture card (Part A of the worksheet) from the Warmer, and a frequency phrase card (Part D).

2 Explain that this indicates what exercise or sport they do, and how often they do it. Explain that they are going to ask everyone in the class what sport or exercise they do and how often they do it. Elicit/teach the questions: *What exercise do you do?* and *How often do you do it?* Demonstrate the exchange.

Student A: What exercise do you do?

Student B: I go jogging.

Student A: How often do you go jogging?

Student B: Twice a week.

3 Explain that when both students have said what exercise they do and how often they do it, they make a note of each other's answers and then find a new partner to speak to. The activity continues in this way until all the students have interviewed everyone in the class.

4 Conduct feedback by asking each student to tell the class about one student they spoke to.

Follow-up

In pairs, students tell each other about the exercise that they do. If they do not do much exercise, they can talk about the exercise someone they know does.

See page 125–6 for the best games from the CD-ROM to play after this unit.

A Pictures

B Word trees

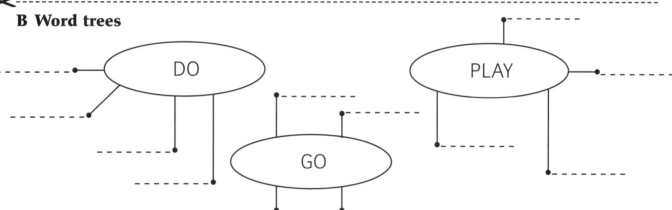

C Group 1 questions

1 Does he do much exercise?
2 How often does he go to the gym?
3 How often does he play tennis?
4 When does he go jogging?
5 How often does he play football?
6 How often does he do aerobics?

Group 2 questions

1 How often does he do yoga?
2 How often does he play hockey?
3 How often does he play golf?
4 How often does he go swimming?
5 How often does he go riding?
6 How often does he do karate?

D Frequency phrases

once a week	twice a week	three times a week	once a month
every day	every weekend	twice a month	three times a month

The beautiful game

LEVEL
Intermediate

ACTIVITY TYPE
Reading
Auction
Writing a report

PREPARATION
One copy of the text and collocation definitions (Part A of the worksheet) for each student
One copy of the auction sentences (Part B) for each student
A class who like football!

TARGET COLLOCATIONS
come on as a substitute,
gain possession,
get off to a good start,
hit the crossbar,
hold your lead,
home advantage,
injury time,
long-range shot,
pass the ball
record turnout,
score from a penalty,
take the lead,
top goalscorer

TIME
45 minutes – 1 hour

Warmer

Ask the class to tell their partner about the best football match they have ever seen.

Input

1 Ask students if they ever read about football matches in the newspaper. Elicit/teach the word *report*.

2 Have students work individually. Give each student a copy of part A of the worksheet. Ask them to read the text (a match report). Ask them *Who won the game?* and *When was the winning goal scored?*

3 Check answers.

> **Answer key**
>
> **1** Cambridge Rovers   **2** in the final minutes of the game

4 Ask the students to read the report and to find the collocations in the report that match the definitions. Ask them to underline those phrases.

5 Check answers.

> **Answer key**
>
> **1** home advantage   **2** record turnout   **3** get off to a great start   **4** long-range shot   **5** hit the crossbar   **6** gain possession   **7** top goalscorer   **8** come on as a substitute   **9** score from a penalty   **10** take the lead   **11** pass the ball   **12** hold the lead   **13** injury time

Practice

1 Make sure that the students can't see a copy of the match report from the Input. (You may like to collect these in while you do this activity.)

2 Talk about what happens at an auction, teaching the phrasal verb *bid for something* or the phrase *make a bid for something*.

3 Tell the students to imagine they have 5000 euros, or the equivalent in their currency, to spend at the auction.

4 Put students in pairs. Give each pair a copy of Part B of the worksheet. They have to look at the sentences and try to decide which are the correct sentences. Then they should decide what they are prepared to bid in order to buy as many sentences as possible. Ask the pairs to decide on their maximum bid for each sentence, writing it in the 'maximum bid' column. The lowest bid they can make is 200 euros.

5 To begin the auction, read out the sentences one at a time and ask for bids. Sell each sentence to the highest bidder. Ask the highest bidder to note down in the last column how much they paid.

6 When all the sentences have been sold, go through the list and tell students whether each sentence was correct or not. Elicit the correct form where the sentence is incorrect.

7 The winners are the pair who bought the most correct sentences.

> **Answer key**
>
> The incorrect sentences are:
>
> **1** shoot (shot)   **3** held a lead (held their lead)   **5** enter as (come on as)   **6** first (top)   **7** got up to (got off to)   **9** posession (possession)   **11** got the lead (took the lead)

Follow-up

Ask the students in pairs to write a report of a football match (real or imagined).

● See page 125–6 for the best games from the CD-ROM to play after this unit.

A Read the text.

Rovers return victorious

If you missed this Saturday's game between Oxford Town and Cambridge Rovers, you missed the match of the season. Oxford, of course, had the home advantage and there was a record turnout of twenty thousand fans. The game got off to a great start. Just three minutes into the first half, Jamie Jackson scored with a spectacular long-range shot. Then ten minutes later, he almost scored again, but this time the ball hit the crossbar. For the rest of the first half, Cambridge struggled to gain possession though a strong defence meant that they stopped Oxford from scoring again.

The second half, however, was a different matter. Within five minutes, Oxford's Paul Taylor (their top goalscorer last season) went off with a leg injury and Sami Ahmed came on as a substitute. Shortly after, Cambridge's Shane Mathers scored from a penalty following a foul against Dean Michael. A great save halfway through the second half by Oxford's Ian Jones prevented Cambridge from taking the lead, but in the final minutes of the game, Cambridge's Mark Hampson passed the ball to Mathers who scored with a glorious volley. Cambridge managed to hold their 2–1 lead through five minutes of injury time. It was a great result for the away team.

Find collocations in the text that mean:

1 the greater chance of success because a team is playing at its own ground
2 the most people that have ever been at a particular event
3 to start very well
4 when a ball is kicked towards the goal from a long way away
5 to hit the post at the top of a goal
6 to win the ball from the other team
7 the person in the team who has scored the most goals
8 when a player replaces another player in the middle of the match
9 to score a goal after being given an advantage because the other team has broken a rule
10 to start to be in the winning position
11 to kick the ball to someone on your team
12 to stay in the winning position
13 minutes added to the end of a game because some time was lost during the game when a player was hurt

B Auction

Sentences for auction	Maximum bid	Price paid
1 The match was won with a long-range shoot from Harley.		
2 Rooney scored from a penalty.		
3 Japan held a lead in the final minutes of the game.		
4 Six minutes of injury time were added to the game.		
5 Didier had to enter as a substitute.		
6 He's the team's first goalscorer.		
7 The match got up to a good start with an early goal from Green.		
8 He passed the ball to the striker.		
9 England failed to gain posession of the ball.		
10 Bayern Munich, of course, had the home advantage.		
11 Just three minutes into the game, Juventus got the lead.		
12 There was more frustration for United as the second shot hit the crossbar.		
13 With over 60,000 fans in attendance, this is surely a record turnout.		

17.3

Champions past and present

LEVEL
Advanced

ACTIVITY TYPE
Text substitution
Role play

MATERIALS
A copy of the
worksheet for each
student

**TARGET
COLLOCATIONS**
all-time great,
caps for his/her
country,
defend a title,
dogged by injury,
drop *someone* from
the team,
fitness levels,
in straight sets,
loss of form,
maintain fitness,
push yourself to the
limit,
reigning champion,
serve an ace,
spent force,
sprained ankle,
the performance of
a lifetime,

TIME
45 minutes – 1 hour

Warmer

Who is your favourite sports star, past or present, and for what reasons do you admire them?

Input

1   Have students working individually. Give each student a copy of the worksheet. Explain that the worksheet contains two texts about two different sports stars. Ask students to read the two texts. Using the questions for each text, students should identify the collocations that give us the main information in the exercises.

2   Ask students to compare their answers to the questions with a partner.

3   Check answers, and write the target collocations (in bold in the answer key below) on the board. (NB you could do this activity as a listening comprehension instead, by giving the students only the exercises and reading the texts aloud as radio reports.)

4   Now do the same for Text B.

> **Answer key**
>
> **A**
> 1   she is destined to become an **all-time great**
> 2   who **pushes herself to the limit**
> 3   she has extraordinary **fitness levels**
> 4   her knack for **serving aces**
> 5   she put on **the performance of a lifetime**
> 6   to defeat the **reigning champion**
> 7   beating Savannah Silva **in straight sets**
> 8   watching her **defend** her new **title** in June
>
> **B**
> 1   had been **dropped from the** national **team**
> 2   has 96 **caps for his country**
> 3   cited **loss of form** as the reason for Havers's omission
> 4   Havers is a **spent force**
> 5   in recent months his career has been **dogged by injury**
> 6   a **sprained ankle**
> 7   hard for him to **maintain fitness**

Practice

1   Put students in pairs and ask each pair to prepare a role play. In the first of these, student A will be Rebecca Jones and student B will be the interviewer, and in the second, student B will be Owen Havers and student A the interviewer. Explain that the interviewers should use the texts to prepare some probing questions, based on the information in the texts.

2   When the pairs have prepared their questions, have them act out the two role plays in turn.

Follow-up

Ask the students to write up the results of their interview with the sports star in the style of an article for a newspaper.

See page 125–6 for the best games from the CD-ROM to play after this unit.

Text A

Read the text about Rebecca Jones and identify the words and phrases that tell us that:

1 Rebecca Jones could be one of the greatest players ever.
2 she works as hard as she possibly can.
3 she is physically very strong and healthy.
4 she often wins points when she is serving.
5 she played better than she has ever played before at Wimbledon last year.
6 her opponent won Wimbledon the year before.
7 her opponent did not win any sets.
8 She will be playing at Wimbledon again this year.

Rebecca Jones, tennis superstar

Rebecca Jones's reputation in the world of tennis is long established but after one of the best seasons of the open era, can anyone now doubt that she is destined to become an all-time great? This is an athlete who pushes herself to the limit. Her training sessions, which start at five o'clock six mornings a week, are nothing short of punishing. Accordingly, she has extraordinary fitness levels that would astound medical science. No other female tennis player can match her speed on court or her knack for serving aces. In the Wimbledon finals last year she put on the performance of a lifetime to defeat the reigning champion, beating Savannah Silva in straight sets. We look forward to watching her defend her new title this summer.

Text B

Read the text about Owen Havers and identify the words and phrases that tell us that:

1 Owen Havers has not been chosen to play in the next international match.
2 he has played almost 100 games for the national team.
3 he has not playing as well as usually recently.
4 he may not play as well ever again.
5 he has had a lot of injuries recently.
6 he hurt a joint in his leg.
7 it has been difficult for him to stay strong and healthy.

Owen Havers, football superstar

Owen Havers scored twice for Juventus in midweek but his joy was short-lived. Yesterday it was announced that the England captain had been dropped from the national team for the first time in a decade. The 31-year-old, who has 96 caps for his country, will not be playing in next week's friendly away to Italy. Haussman, England's manager, cited loss of form as the reason for Havers's omission. It has even been suggested in some quarters that Havers is a spent force. Certainly, in recent months, his career has been dogged by injury. A sprained ankle in June of this year made it hard for him to maintain fitness over the summer. Let's see how he fares this season before we write him off for good.

18.1

Free-time fun

LEVEL
Elementary /
Pre-intermediate

ACTIVITY TYPE
Free-time activity
survey

MATERIALS
One copy of the
words and grid (Part
A of the worksheet)
for each student
One of the cut-up
cards from part B
for each student

**TARGET
COLLOCATIONS**
go out with friends,
go to a concert,
go to a film,
go to a museum,
go to the cinema,
go to the theatre,
listen to a concert,
listen to music,
listen to the radio,
play music,
play computer games,
read a book,
read a magazine,
read a newspaper,
read poetry,
watch a film,
watch TV

TIME
45 minutes – 1 hour

Warmer

1 Write the word *book* on a piece of paper and show it to one student. Ask him or her to mime or draw it for the other students to guess.

2 Continue the game with other students and the following words: *cinema, concert, film, magazine, museum, music, newspaper, poetry, radio, theatre, TV, friends, computer games.*

Input

1 Give each student a copy of Part A of the worksheet. Ask students to add the words in the appropriate spaces in the table.

2 Ask students to compare answers with a partner.

3 Check answers, drawing attention to the use / non-use of the definite and indefinite articles. Avoid giving any grammatical explanations, but recommend that students learn these as part of the collocation.

> **Answer key**
>
> going out with friends
>
> going to the cinema / a concert / a film / a museum / the theatre
>
> listening to a concert / music / the radio
>
> playing computer games/music
>
> reading a book/a magazine / the newspaper / poetry
>
> watching a film/TV

Practice

1 Ask students which of the things they like doing and elicit/teach *I like playing computer games / going to the cinema*, etc. Elicit/teach the question form *Do you like playing computer games / going to the cinema?* Write the structure on the board.

2 Give each student one of the cards (Part B of the worksheet) and explain that a tick indicates what they like doing, and a cross indicates what they don't like doing. Explain that for each free-time activity they should find another person who has the same like/ dislike. If there are 14 or more students in the class, they should write a different name for each activity. If there are between 7 and 14 students, they should not write the same name more than twice.

3 Monitor for the correct use of the collocations as students mingle.

4 Conduct feedback, asking students to report back on what they found out.

Follow-up

1 Put students into groups of three.

2 Ask each student to write out the list of collocations in order of personal preference (secretly so that the other students in their group cannot see it).

3 Explain that the students in each group should take it in turns to try and guess the order of preference of the other students in the group.

● See page 125–6 for the best games from the CD-ROM to play after this unit.

A Write the words in the box in the correct space in the table.

> a book, the cinema, computer games, a concert, a film, friends, a magazine, a museum, music, the newspaper, poetry, the radio, the theatre, TV

going out with	
going to	
listening to	
playing	
reading	
watching	

✂ -

B Cards

radio ✗	theatre ✗	music ✓	book ✓
newspaper ✓	poetry ✓	book ✓	concert ✗
concert ✓	book ✗	concert ✓	theatre ✗
museum ✓	music ✗	TV ✓	poetry ✗
theatre ✗	museum ✗	cinema ✗	music ✗
poetry ✓	radio ✓	film ✗	TV ✓
cinema ✗	tv ✗	magazine ✗	museum ✗
film ✓	concert ✗	computer games ✓	newspaper ✗
magazine ✗	newspaper ✓	friends ✗	radio ✓
computer games ✗	cinema ✓	museum ✓	magazine ✓
friends ✓	magazine ✓	theatre ✗	film ✗
TV ✗	film ✓	poetry ✗	friends ✗
music ✓	friends ✓	radio ✗	computer games ✗
book ✗	computer games ✓	newspaper ✗	cinema ✓

18.2

LEVEL
Intermediate

ACTIVITY TYPE
Reading
Writing

MATERIALS
One copy of the collocations and definitions (Part A of the worksheet), cut up into cards and shuffled, for each pair
One copy of the two mini-biographies (Part B) for each student

TARGET COLLOCATIONS
a film comes out,
box-office hit,
catchy tune,
direct a movie,
give a performance,
go on tour,
good reviews,
greatest hits,
happy ending,
live music,
opening scene,
play a role,
release an album,
star in a film

TIME
45 minutes – 1 hour

Star quality

Warmer

Discuss what sort of films and music the students like to watch or listen to.

Input

1   Put students in pairs and give them a set of collocation and definition cards (Part A of the worksheet), mixed up. Ask them to match each collocation to its definition.

2   Check answers. Explain that *movie* and *film* are synonyms and they can both be used in these collocations.

3   Ask students to sort the collocations into those which refer to film, those which refer to music and those which refer to both.

> **Answer key**
>
> **Film**: a film comes out, star in a film, play a role, direct a movie, opening scenes, box-office hit, have a happy ending (this could also refer to music as a song that tells a story could have a happy ending)
>
> **Music**: live music, go on tour, catchy tune, release an album, greatest hits
>
> **Both**: good reviews, give a performance

Practice

1   Give each student a copy of the two texts (Part B of the worksheet). Explain that the two texts are mini-biographies of an actor and a musician. Ask the students to read the texts and find the words and phrases that mean the same as the collocations they have just read, and underline them.

2   Ask students to compare answers with a partner.

3   Ask students to work in pairs to replace the underlined phrases with the collocations.

Answer key

To be underlined ...	... and replaced with ...
acting the part	playing the role of
very beginning of the film	opening scenes
play big parts	star
was in charge of	directed
watched by millions of people in cinemas	a box-office hit
end with something good happening	have a happy ending
will be in cinemas	comes out in
music that is played in front of audiences	live music
travelled to play in several different places	went on tour
tunes that are easy to remember	catchy tunes
praise from newspaper and magazine writers	good review
play at a concert	give a performance
in the shops	released
most popular songs	greatest hits

Follow-up

Write a mini-biography of a world-famous actor or musician. Exchange it with someone else and try to guess who it is.

● See page 125–6 for the best games from the CD-ROM to play after this unit.

A Collocation and definition cards

a film comes out	a film can be seen for the first time in cinemas
star in a film	to be one of the most important actors in a film
play a role	to act the part of a particular person in a film or play
direct a movie	to be in charge of a movie and tell the actors what to do
opening scenes	the very first part of a film
have a happy ending	when the story ends with something good happening
box-office hit	a film that lots of people go to see at the cinema
live music	music that is played on instruments to an audience
go on tour	to play several concerts in a row in different towns and cities
catchy tune	a tune that is easy to remember
good reviews	when people write good things about music, films, books, etc.
give a performance	to play music, dance, sing or act in front of an audience
release an album	to make a record, CD, etc. that is sold to the public
greatest hits	a musician or group's most popular songs

B Read the texts and underline the phrases that can be replaced by the collocations in Part A.

Harry Hall

The legendary actor and director of horror movies Harry Hall has died in his Hollywood mansion at the age of 78. Hall began his career as a child actor, acting the part of Ben in the popular film *Last Train to Basel*. He charmed audiences from the very beginning of the film, in which he was filmed wandering through the mountains with his trusty dog Buttons. He went on to play big parts in many films, but he is best known for his horror films. He was in charge of his first horror movie, *The Phantom*, in 1957, and it was watched by millions of people in cinemas worldwide. Although he rejected the Hollywood idea that every movie should end with something good happening, he was extremely successful. His last movie, which he was working on up to his death, will be in cinemas in September.

Gloria Grisoni

Gloria Grisoni has been a champion of music that is played in front of audiences for all of her long and successful career. She and her glamorous band of backing singers and dancers travelled to play in several different places for the fist time in 1975, and she has hardly stopped travelling since. Her songs are a popular combination of strong dance rhythms and tunes and are easy to remember. They have earned her praise from newspaper and magazine writers from Amsterdam to Zanzibar and hundreds of places in between. She was even invited to play at a concert to celebrate the release of Nelson Mandela in 1990. Grisoni's next album will be for sale in the shops this week, while a compilation CD of all her most popular songs has already sold more than 3 million copies.

18.3

Critics' corner

LEVEL
Advanced

ACTIVITY TYPE
Reading
Text substitution
Writing

MATERIALS
One copy of
collocations box A
for half the students
and one copy of
collocations box B for
the other half of the
students
One copy of the
reviews (Part C of
the worksheet) for
every student

**TARGET
COLLOCATIONS**
all-star cast,
an eye for detail,
bold experiment,
compulsive reading,
dazzling display,
fire *someone's*
imagination,
glowing reviews,
haunting melody,
lasting impression,
massive hit,
spectacularly
successful,
startling originality,
thrilling finale,
unmitigated disaster,
virtuoso performance

TIME
45 minutes – 1 hour

Warmer

Ask students to tell each other about the last film they saw or the last concert they went to, and what they liked or disliked about it.

Input

1   Put students in pairs. Give half collocation box A and the other half box B. Refer students to the example. Ask them to decide which is the correct definition for *bold experiment* (answer: a).

2   Explain that half the class have one set of six collocations and the other half have a different set.

3   Explain that for each collocation they should write a correct definition and an incorrect definition on a separate piece of paper (using a dictionary if necessary). They should write each collocation and the definitions on a separate piece of paper and vary the order of the definitions so that the correct one is not always given first.

4   When they have finished, each pair should swap sheets with a pair who has the other set of collocations, and try to identify the correct definitions.

5   Ask students to swap the papers back for marking.

6   Conduct feedback, and make sure everyone understands the collocations.

Practice

1   Give each student a copy of the three reviews all written by a grumpy arts critic (Part C of the worksheet).

2   Explain that students should identify and underline the sections of the text that express the *opposite* view to the sentences/phrases below each text.

3   Check answers.

> **Answer key**
> 1   In fact, two days after reading it, I have managed to delete most of it from my mind.
> 2   … his dull prose and formulaic structure will not win him new readers.
> 3   Dagger is shockingly slack on detail.
> 4   At times, watching paint dry would have been more fun than reading this book …
> 5   If it wasn't my job, I would never have made it as far as the predictable and uninspired ending.
> 6   It was one of those films that you feel you've seen a hundred times before.
> 7   Reviews have been lukewarm …
> 8   The actors (none of whom are well known) …
> 9   … the idea of setting the story in Egypt was an unmitigated disaster.
> 10 The songs, specially composed by Donny Duo, were instantly forgettable, …
> 11 … the show's so-called 'climax' was an uninspired ice-skating routine on a tiny ice rink constructed on the stage.
> 12 I left the theatre with my brain feeling sluggish from an evening of mediocrity.
> 13 Camille Cabaret gives a lacklustre performance as Yvette, the showgirl.

4   In pairs, the students should choose one of the reviews (play, book or film) and write a positive review of it.

Follow-up

Ask students to write about a film they have seen, a theatre performance they have been to or a book they have read, and to use some of the collocations from the lesson.

🔘 See page 125–6 for the best games from the CD-ROM to play after this unit.

A

compulsive reading	a lasting impression	a eye for detail
a thrilling finale	glowing reviews	an all star cast

Example: A **bold experiment** is: a) an attempt to do something unusual and interesting.
                                                  b) an experiment that should only be attempted by scientists.

- -

B

startling originality	something spectacularly successful	unmitigated disaster
virtuoso performance	haunting melody	massive hit

Example: A **bold experiment** is: a) an attempt to do something unusual and interesting.
       b)   an experiment that should only be attempted by scientists.

- -

C 1

The Ace of Spades by Alvin Dagger

At times, watching paint dry would have been more fun than reading this book – the over-long, over-hyped latest novel from crime writer Alvin Dagger. Dagger is shockingly slack on detail: his detectives struggle on with vague descriptions and unexplained motives. If it wasn't my job, I would never have made it as far as the predictable and uninspired ending. In fact, two days after reading it, I have managed to delete most of it from my mind. Someone should tell Mr Dagger that crime writing has moved on: his dull prose and formulaic structure will not win him new readers.

1   The book made a **lasting impression on me.**
2   This **bold experiment** in crime writing is sure to win Mr Dagger new readers.
3   Dagger has a real **eye for detail**.
4   The latest novel from crime writer Alvin Dagger is **compulsive reading**.

2

The Grass Whispers, directed by Georgina Gearing

Reviews have been lukewarm and box-office receipts small for Georgina Gearing's latest film. Nevertheless I was optimistic as I settled down in the cinema, as I greatly enjoyed her first two films. What a disappointment. The actors (none of whom are well known) were wooden and unconvincing, and the idea of setting the story in Egypt was an unmitigated disaster. As for the plot, well, there was never any doubt about what would happen next. It was one of those films that you feel you've seen a hundred times before.

5   I could hardly put the book down before I reached the **thrilling finale**.
6   It was a film of **startling originality**.
7   Her films have received **glowing reviews**.
8   The film has an **all-star cast**.
9   The idea of setting the story in Egypt is **spectacularly successful**.

3

The Last Show on Earth at the Playhouse Theatre

This play is billed as a 'heart-stopping spectacle of theatre, dance and music'. The only thing about it that stopped my heart was the price of the tickets. Camille Cabaret gives a lacklustre performance as Yvette, the showgirl. The songs, specially composed by Donny Duo, were instantly forgettable, and the show's so-called 'climax' was an uninspired ice-skating routine on a tiny ice rink constructed on the stage. I left the theatre with my brain feeling sluggish from an evening of mediocrity. This show is sure to be yet another disaster for the Playhouse Theatre.

10   The **haunting melodies** were specially composed by Donny Duo.
11   The show's climax was a **dazzling display** of ice-skating on a special rink constructed on the stage.
12   I left the theatre feeling that the show had really **fired my imagination**.
13   Camille Cabaret gives a **virtuoso performance** as Yvette, the showgirl.

Wordlists

1 Everyday activities

1.1 What we do
call a friend
catch the bus
clean your teeth
have a shower
have breakfast
listen to music
make dinner
meet a friend
read the paper
watch television

1.2 The routines game
check your email
do the housework
do the ironing
do the washing-up
draw the curtains
fall asleep
get dressed/undressed
go out for dinner
lay the table
lock the door
make the bed
open the blinds
pay the bills
turn on the TV

1.3 A day in the life
alarm clock goes off
call in sick
catch up on sleep
clear up a mess
get off to sleep
pick up a bargain
soak up the sun
stay out late
strike up a conversation
work up an appetite

2 Families and relationships

2.1 This is your life
best friend
big family
fall in love
get divorced
get married
happy marriage
have children
leave home
live together
make friends

2.2 Best of friends
circle of friends
close family
close friend
enjoy *someone's* company
form a friendship
frosty reception
get in touch
keep in touch
lose touch

old friend
stay in touch
warm welcome

2.3 Love story
end in divorce
fairytale wedding
fight for custody
gain custody
immediate family
love at first sight
messy divorce
mutual friend
pay maintenance
propose marriage
set up home
throw a party

3 Communicating

3.1 It's good to talk
get a letter
get a phone call
get a text
get an email
have a chat
have an argument
make a phone call
send a letter
send a text
send an email

3.2 Talking sense
say goodbye
say hello
say sorry
say your prayers
speak your mind
talk nonsense
talk sense
tell a joke
tell a lie
tell a story
tell the truth

3.3 You're making it up!
apologise profusely
ask a favour
backhanded compliment
drop a hint
exchange pleasantries
feeble excuse
fish for compliments
hazard a guess
pay *someone* a compliment
pick a fight
rash promise
sweeping generalisation
tentative suggestion
wild accusation

4 Describing people

4.1 Who am I?
bald head
big nose
curly hair
dark hair

dark skin
fair hair
fair skin
have a beard
have a moustache
long hair
short hair
straight hair
wear a hat
wear glasses

4.2 Wanted!
bald patch
broad shoulders
broken teeth
bushy eyebrows
cheeky grin
chubby cheeks
full lips
heavy build
lined face
long eyelashes
long nose
narrow shoulders
pointed chin
shoulder-length hair
slim build

4.3 Find a friend
boundless energy
deeply religious
downright rude
good listener
good sense of humour
highly opinionated
impeccable manners
infectious laugh
keen interest
of average intelligence
outgoing personality
painfully shy
physically fit
ready wit
show consideration
strong personality

5 Emotions

5.1 Feelings
feel angry
feel bored
feel excited
feel happy
feel lonely
feel pleased
feel sad
feel upset
make *someone* angry
make *someone* cry
make *someone* happy
make *someone* laugh
make *someone* sad
make *someone* smile

5.2 Consequences
be absolutely delighted
be in a bad mood
be in a good mood

be wildly excited
be worried sick
burst into tears
burst out laughing
drive *someone* crazy
drive *someone* mad
get a real buzz
hurt *someone's* feelings
jump for joy
lose your temper

5.3 Dominoes
bitterly/deeply disappointed
blissfully happy
bored stiff
bored out of your mind
deeply distressed
deeply offended
deeply/profoundly depressed
deeply/profoundly shocked
highly amused
highly irritated
insanely jealous
intensely irritated
madly in love
mildly amused
mildly depressed
mildly irritated
profoundly grateful

6 Studying and learning

6.1 A life of learning
do a course
do your homework
go to college
go to school
go to university
leave school
pass/fail an exam
start school
take an exam
write an essay

6.2 Which school?
carry out experiments
complete your studies
continue your studies
do project work
enrol on a course
get bored
good sports facilities
hand in your work
learn *something* by heart
natural talent
pay attention
play truant
quick learner

6.3 A good education
attend lectures
background reading
continuous assessment
drop out of university
formal qualifications
gifted children
give feedback
marked improvement

mixed-ability class
raise standards
room for improvement
vocational training
your attention wanders

7 Problems and solutions

7.1 A bad day
call the helpdesk
car won't start
computer crashes
find your house keys
have a headache
late for work
lose your house keys
miss the train
take a tablet
take a taxi
wait for the (next) train
work/stay late

7.2 If I were you …
a range of options
a tough choice
a wide choice
bear in mind
consider a possibility
consider the options
keep in mind
seriously consider
the obvious choice
the only option
think long and hard
your best option

7.3 Problems at work
fill vacancies
high absence rates
inappropriate dress
job satisfaction
job security
low morale
low productivity rates
motivate staff
people skills
poor performance
poor time management
recruit staff
retain staff
stress-related illness
unprofessional attitude

8 Food and drink

8.1 Going shopping
bar of chocolate
bottle of water
bottle of wine
bunch of bananas
bunch of grapes
carton of milk
carton of yoghurt
jar of coffee
jar of jam
loaf of bread
packet of biscuits

packet of sweets
tin of tomatoes

8.2 Let's cook!
add the tomatoes
break the eggs
bring some water to the boil
chop the onions
cook the pasta
cream the butter and sugar
drain the pasta
heat the oil
melt the chocolate
sift the flour
skin the tomatoes
spread the mixture
whisk the eggs

8.3 Restaurant reviews
à la carte menu
creamy sauce
crisp pastry
efficient service
fresh ingredients
greasy chips
inflated prices
instant coffee
limp salad
relaxed atmosphere
rich dessert
seasonal vegetables
set menu
short-staffed
soggy vegetables
subtle lighting
vegetarian option

9 Travel

9.1 Travel survey
catch a bus
catch a boat
catch a ferry
catch a plane
catch a train
drive a bus
drive a car
drive a tractor
get/take a bus
get/take a coach
get/take a plane
get/take a taxi
get/take a train
go by bus/car
go by bike/motorbike
go by taxi/train
go on foot
ride a bike/motorbike

9.2 Going for a drive
brake sharply
car breaks down
change gear
dip your headlights
give *someone* a lift
heavy traffic
increase speed
look in the mirror

lose your licence
read the map
sound the horn
start the engine
wear a seatbelt

9.3 Further afield
board a plane
break your journey
connecting flight
go through security
internal flight
issue *someone* with a boarding card
long-haul flight
pass through passport control
point of departure
reclaim your baggage
short-haul flight
travel light

10 Health and medicine

10.1 Doctor, doctor
break your arm
break your leg
call an ambulance
feel sick
have (got) a cold
have an operation
go into hospital
leave hospital
take a tablet
take medicine

10.2 In good health
check *someone's* blood pressure
dull ache
fall ill
feel *someone's* pulse
heavy cold
make an appointment
runny nose
sharp pain
sore throat
splitting headache
take *someone's* temperature
write a prescription

10.3 A healthy mind
admit someone to hospital
adverse reaction
dress a wound
experience side effects
heavily sedated
in a critical condition
in a stable condition
infectious disease
sprain your ankle
symptoms persist
take an overdose
undergo treatment

11 Work

11.1 The world of work
a high salary
a low salary
be badly paid

be well paid
earn money
get a new job
have an interview
look for a job
lose your job
work hard

11.2 Overworked?
apply for a job
demanding work
give up a job
heavy workload
highly qualified
join a company
leave a company
long hours
member of staff
reach a target
set up a business
suffer from stress

Unit 11.3 Work stories
a high turnover of staff
hand in your notice
highly motivated
high-powered job
land a job
lay off staff
manual labour
menial task
on-the-job training
seek promotion
take on staff
unpaid overtime
unsocial hours

12 Money

12.1 Money money money!
borrow money
earn money
get paid
lend money
make money
pay a bill
pay by credit card
pay tax
pay the rent
save money
spend money
take credit cards

12.2 Short of money
annual salary
bring in money
careful with money
get a loan
have an overdraft
highly paid
leave a tip
make a living
owe money
pay interest
pay off a loan
pay well
poorly paid
steady income

12.3 Good with money
bargain hunting
big-ticket item
cost a fortune
dirt cheap
expensive tastes
false economy
hard-earned cash
part with your cash
pay over the odds
spend a fortune
value for money

13 Where we live

13.1 Leaving home
do the housework
feel homesick
get home
house-warming party
leave home
live next door
live on your own
move house
rent a house
share a house

13.2 Room to let
block of flats
fitted kitchen
friendly neighbourhood
fully furnished
nicely furnished
off-street parking
overlook the garden
residential area
shared house
spacious room
studio flat
within walking distance of
(the station, etc.)

13.3 A better place to live
affordable housing
antisocial behaviour
deprived area
due for demolition
housing stock
human habitation
inner-city area
littered pavements
local amenities
low-income families
recycling facilities
sense of community
underage drinking

14 Crime and punishment

14.1 Call the police!
a serious crime
call the police
commit a crime
go to prison
pay a fine
police arrest *someone*

rob a bank
spend x years/months in prison
steal a bike
steal a car

14.2 We have reached a verdict ...
be found guilty
be guilty of a crime
be on the scene
be sentenced to X years in prison
be severely punished
begin a prison sentence
break into a house
criminal record
plead guilty
reach a verdict
report something/someone to the police
serve a sentence

14.3 Does the punishment fit the crime?
act as a deterrent
behind bars
carry a sentence
condone someone's actions
extenuating circumstances
get off lightly
hardened criminal
hefty sentence
law-abiding citizen
lenient sentence
previous convictions
show remorse
stiff penalty
unprovoked attack

15 Modern technology

15.1 Home computer
check your email
copy text
create a new document
do a search
go online
lose your work
new message
online shopping
save a document
send an email
start up a computer
visit a website

15.2 Help – it won't work!
a password expires
an email bounces
delete a file
enter a password
forward an email
install software
open an attachment
print out a document
read an attachment
restart a computer
run software
shut down a computer

15.3 What do you use yours for?
archive your documents
back up your work
bookmark a site
create an avatar
debug a program
download a podcast
download music
format a document
install an application
make a hard copy
navigate a website
position the cursor
resize a window
write code
zip/unzip a file

16 The natural world

16.1 Wish you were here
bright sunshine
calm sea
dark clouds
heavy rain
high mountains
sandy beach
snow falls
steep hill
strong winds
thick fog

16.2 Disaster!
boat capsizes
bring chaos
bring down cables
cause damage
experience difficulties
extreme weather conditions
icy waters
radio for help
rain heavily
rivers burst their banks
rough sea
struck by lightning
towns are cut off
violent storms
widespread flooding

16.3 Adventure travel
blanket of fog
dense forest
fast-flowing river
fog lifts
gusty winds
hard frost
heavy seas
panoramic views
rolling hills
rugged mountains
secluded beach
stifling heat
storm abates
torrential rain
tropical island

17 Sport and exercise

17.1 What do you do?
do aerobics
do karate
do sport/exercise
do yoga
go jogging
go riding
go swimming
go to the gym
play football
play golf
play hockey
play tennis

17.2 The beautiful game
come on as a substitute
gain possession
get off to a good start
hit the crossbar
hold your lead
home advantage
injury time
long-range shot
pass the ball
record turnout
score from a penalty
take the lead
top goalscorer

17.3 Champions past and present
all-time great
caps for his/her country
defend a title
dogged by injury
drop someone from the team
fitness levels
in straight sets
loss of form
maintain fitness
push yourself to the limit
reigning champion
serve an ace
spent force
sprained ankle
the performance of a lifetime

18 Leisure activities

18.1 Free-time fun
go out with friends
go to a concert
go to a film
go to a museum
go to the cinema
go to the theatre
listen to a concert
listen to music
listen to the radio
play computer games
play music
read a book
read a magazine
read a newspaper

read poetry
watch a film
watch TV/(the) television

18.2 Star quality
a film comes out
box-office hit
catchy tune
direct a movie
give a performance
go on tour
good reviews
greatest hits
happy ending
live music
opening scene
play a role
release an album
star in a film

18.3 Critics' corner
All-star cast
an eye for detail
bold experiment
compulsive reading
dazzling display
fire *someone's* imagination
glowing reviews
haunting melody
lasting impression
massive hit
spectacularly successful
startling originality
thrilling finale
unmitigated disaster
virtuoso performance

Check the table to see which games are most appropriate for the unit your students have studied.

Unit Number	Topic	Level	Dominoes	Pelmanism	What's the collocation?
1.1	Everyday Activities	Elementary / Pre-intermediate	✔	✔	✔
1.2	Everyday Activities	Intermediate	✔	✔	✔
1.3	Everyday Activities	Advanced	✔	✔	✔
2.1	Families and relationships	Elementary / Pre-intermediate	✔	✔	✔
2.2	Families and relationships	Intermediate	✔	✔	✔
2.3	Families and relationships	Advanced	✔	✔	✔
3.1	Communicating	Elementary / Pre-intermediate	✘	✘	✔
3.2	Communicating	Intermediate	✔	✔	✔
3.3	Communicating	Advanced	✔	✔	✔
4.1	Describing people	Elementary / Pre-intermediate	✔	✔	✔
4.2	Describing people	Intermediate	✔	✔	✔
4.3	Describing people	Advanced	✔	✔	✔
5.1	Emotions and feelings	Elementary / Pre-intermediate	✘	✘	✔
5.2	Emotions and feelings	Intermediate	✔	✔	✔
5.3	Emotions and feelings	Advanced	✔	✔	✔
6.1	Studying and learning	Elementary / Pre-intermediate	✔	✔	✔
6.2	Studying and learning	Intermediate	✔	✔	✔
6.3	Studying and learning	Advanced	✔	✔	✔
7.1	Problems and solutions	Elementary / Pre-intermediate	✔	✔	✔
7.2	Problems and solutions	Intermediate	✔	✔	✔
7.3	Problems and solutions	Advanced	✔	✔	✔
8.1	Food and drink	Elementary / Pre-intermediate	✔	✔	✔
8.2	Food and drink	Intermediate	✔	✔	✔
8.3	Food and drink	Advanced	✔	✔	✔
9.1	Travel	Elementary / Pre-intermediate	✔	✔	✘
9.2	Travel	Intermediate	✔	✔	✔
9.3	Travel	Advanced	✔	✔	✔

Unit Number	Topic	Level	Dominoes	Pelmanism	What's the collocation?
10.1	Health and medicine	Elementary / Pre-intermediate	✔	✔	✔
10.2	Health and medicine	Intermediate	✔	✔	✔
10.3	Health and medicine	Advanced	✔	✔	✔
11.1	Work	Elementary / Pre-intermediate	✔	✔	✔
11.2	Work	Intermediate	✔	✔	✔
11.3	Work	Advanced	✔	✔	✔
12.1	Money	Elementary / Pre-intermediate	✔	✔	✔
12.2	Money	Intermediate	✔	✔	✔
12.3	Money	Advanced	✔	✔	✔
13.1	Where we live	Elementary / Pre-intermediate	✔	✔	✔
13.2	Where we live	Intermediate	✔	✔	✔
13.3	Where we live	Advanced	✔	✔	✔
14.1	Crime and punishment	Elementary / Pre-intermediate	✔	✔	✔
14.2	Crime and punishment	Intermediate	✔	✔	✔
14.3	Crime and punishment	Advanced	✔	✔	✔
15.1	Modern technology	Elementary / Pre-intermediate	✔	✔	✔
15.2	Modern technology	Intermediate	✔	✔	✔
15.3	Modern technology	Advanced	✔	✔	✔
16.1	The natural world	Elementary / Pre-intermediate	✔	✔	✔
16.2	The natural world	Intermediate	✔	✔	✔
16.3	The natural world	Advanced	✔	✔	✔
17.1	Sport and exercise	Elementary / Pre-intermediate	✔	✔	✔
17.2	Sport and exercise	Intermediate	✔	✔	✔
17.3	Sport and exercise	Advanced	✔	✔	✔
18.1	Leisure activities	Elementary / Pre-intermediate	✔	✔	✔
18.2	Leisure activities	Intermediate	✔	✔	✔
18.3	Leisure activities	Advanced	✔	✔	✔

From *Collocations Extra* by Elizabeth Walter and Kate Woodford © Cambridge University Press 2010 **PHOTOCOPIABLE**